A GIFT FOR

My dear friend
Jacki

÷ FROM ÷

Ashley

Nov. 30, 2005

50 Simple Ways
to *Pamper*
—— Yourself ——

Edited by Deborah Balmuth and Robin Catalano
Interior illustrations by Carleen Powell
Text design and production by Mary B. Minella
Indexed by Susan Olason, Indexes & Knowledge Maps

The information in this book is true and complete to the best of our
knowledge. All recommendations are made without guarantee on the
part of the author or Storey Books. The author and publisher disclaim
any liability in connection with the use of this information. For addi-
tional information, please contact Storey Books, Schoolhouse Road,
Pownal, Vermont 05261.

50 Simple Ways

to *Pamper*

—— Yourself ——

Stephanie Tourles

BOK 5016

Contents

Dedication

To my husband, Bill . . . thanks for your strong
shoulders, your never-ending support,
your laughter, your encouragement to explore
my dreams, to push my limits, to find my life's
direction. I love you more and more with
each breath I take, my sweet William.

Acknowledgments

All books start with an idea, a seed. I wish to thank
my editor, Deborah Balmuth, for giving me this seed
and asking me to fertilize it and make it grow. And
many thanks to those of you who most graciously
shared with me your favorite ways to pamper yourselves and improve your health and well-being.

Let Go of the Guilt

The word *pamper* is a verb meaning "to gratify the wishes of, especially by catering to physical comforts." It also means "to spoil, coddle, humor, indulge, or caress." Sounds like pampering is something most of us could use more of in these stressful times.

If you bought this book for yourself, did you feel just a little bit guilty buying a book devoted solely to pampering? Are you afraid that someone will think you're being selfish by wanting to spend some quality time dedicated to boosting your own well-being? Well, chase those thoughts right out of your head. Don't think of pampering yourself as decadence or forbidden pleasure. Think of it as a way to preserve your sanity in an insanely paced world.

We're all so very busy, busy, busy. Buzzing around like worker bees, tending to everyone else's needs and ignoring our own, to a large extent. Do you work all day caring for children or elderly parents, or work outside the home in a 40- to 60-hour-per-week career? Are you a full-time student? Isn't it pure ectasy to know that after you finish all that work, you get to go grocery shopping, cook dinner, do the laundry, clean the house, pay the bills, mow the lawn, fix the car, and meet with the insurance agent? Sure it is! Who needs personal time?

As if life wasn't busy enough before technology exploded onto the scene, now we're expected to be super-people. Living life at breakneck speed can make us feel as if we're on a wild roller-coaster ride that won't stop. We can't continue to work faster and faster and process more and more information and still function as normal, happy, healthy human beings. Needless to say, most of us are frazzled. We need a break … to catch our breath, to regain our health, to restore our natural rhythms, to enjoy the meaningful moments in life that have gone by the wayside because we're so busy. In a word, we need *pampering*.

It's not a dirty word that should make you feel guilty. You deserve a bit of pampering. I'm sure you've earned it.

By pampering yourself, you don't have to take an entire day off and loaf around (though that's advisable from time to time); you can simply integrate small moments of pampering into your everyday life. This book is filled with simple ways to de-stress and unwind, to find more pleasure, more joy, and to look and feel better about yourself. These invaluable tips will help you enjoy more "you" time. When you're happier and calmer, radiant from the inside out, glowing with health and beauty, believe me, those around you will sit up and take notice.

INFORMATION AND CAUTIONS

Most of the ingredients mentioned in this book, including essential oils and herbs, can be found in natural-food or health-food stores. Natural product and herbal mail-order suppliers are also a good place to look.

When using any new ingredient for the first time, it's always best to try a patch test. Apply a bit of the ingredient or formula to the inside of your arm, and allow it to remain for 24 hours. If any signs of allergic response — redness, itching, or other skin irritation — occur, discontinue use immediately. In addition, be sure to use caution in handling pure essential oils. Because they are highly concentrated, they can cause adverse skin reactions. Always use a dropper when measuring essential oils, and do not use more than recommended; more can be dangerous, not better. Keep all ingredients out of the reach of children and pets.

So go ahead, pamper yourself . . . you're worth it!

Blessings of health and happiness to you
and yours,

Stephanie L. Tourles

1

C'mon Get Happy

Remember how you danced and sang as a child, usually in a group of other smiling, laughing children? Can you remember how everyone looked: clear-eyed, with radiant faces and glowing health? Recapture this youthful happiness and low level of stress and you are guaranteed to feel better.

As an added bonus, you'll even look better. Why? Stress restricts blood flow to the skin, preventing moisture and nutrients from getting where they need to go. Stress also promotes the production of the male hormone testosterone, which stimulates oil production. That, in turn, promotes pimple formation and clogged pores. Lowering your stress level will dramatically improve the texture and condition of your skin.

Manage Your Stress

Use lavender essential oil to help you relax; it is a natural sedative and nervine. When I'm about to give a speech and herbal demonstration to a group of people, I still, to this day, get quite nervous. To regain my confident and calm demeanor, I place 3 drops of pure lavender essential oil onto a soft tissue or small handkerchief and inhale deeply of the floral aroma about five times just prior to my presentation. I'm serene within minutes.

Job or family demands getting to you? This exercise sequence works wonders to help you refocus, de-stress, and re-energize:

- Stand up with your feet shoulder width apart, placing your palms on your lower abdomen. Close your eyes and slowly inhale through your nose, gradually expanding your diaphragm. If you're breathing correctly, you will feel your hands move outward. Hold for a count of five, then exhale slowly through your mouth. Do this 10 times.

- Now that you're calmer and have more oxygen circulating throughout your body, place your arms straight out in front of you. Slowly do 10 deep knee bends. Make sure to squeeze your buttocks on the way back up. Don't you feel better now?

Smile more. Even if you're having a bad day, try to find at least one good thing that will bring a smile to your face. Is the sky bright and sunny? Are the birds singing? Are you healthy? Is there fresh snow on the ground? Do you have a beautiful manicure?

Laugh more. "Laughter is the best medicine" — how true that is. Go see a funny movie, read a funny book, play with your children (children are always laughing), or play with your pet. Laughter makes you feel good, makes your skin glow, and stimulates circulation throughout your body. Go ahead — have a good, hearty guffaw!

Get-Happy Herb Tea

When you're at your wit's end and your nerves are jangling, make a cup or two of this soothing, relaxing tea. Happiness and peace of mind are only minutes away. All the herbs in this recipe are dried.

2 cups boiling water
½ teaspoon lemon balm leaves
½ teaspoon chamomile flowers
½ teaspoon lavender flowers
¼ teaspoon passionflower leaves or flowers
½ teaspoon spearmint or peppermint leaves

Remove the pot of boiling water from the heat, add the herbs, cover, and steep for 5 to 10 minutes. Strain. Add honey or lemon to taste, if desired. Sip slowly and enjoy! This tea is also delicious iced for a refreshing summer beverage.

Get Steamed

An herbal facial steam will hydrate your skin and allow your pores to perspire and breathe. As the steam penetrates your skin, the various herbs will soften its surface, act as an astringent, and aid in healing skin lesions. Also, any clogging from dirt or makeup will be loosened for easy removal afterward.

Herbal steams can be used regularly by those with normal, dry, or oily skin. Those of you with sensitive skin, dilated capillaries, rosacea, or sunburned skin, however, should abstain. Always cleanse your skin before steaming.

Steams for Pore Perfection

To prepare a facial steam, boil 4 cups of distilled water (and vinegar, if the recipe calls for it). Remove from the heat, add herbs, cover, and allow to steep for about 5 minutes. Place the pot in a safe, stable place where you can sit comfortably for about 10 minutes. Use a bath towel to create a tent over your head, shoulders, and steaming herb pot; allow 10 to 12 inches between the steaming herb pot and your face to avoid burning your skin. Close your eyes, breathe deeply, and relax.

All the herbs in the following blends are in dried form. If you're using fresh herbs, double the quantity.

For Normal or Oily Skin: 1 teaspoon yarrow, 1 teaspoon sage, 1 teaspoon rosemary, and 1 teaspoon peppermint.

For Normal or Dry Skin: 1 teaspoon orange flowers, 2 teaspoons comfrey leaves, and 1 teaspoon elder flowers.

For All Skin Types: 1 teaspoon calendula, 1 teaspoon chamomile, 1 teaspoon raspberry leaves, 1 teaspoon peppermint, and 1 teaspoon strawberry leaves.

Wrinkle Chaser: 1 tablespoon crushed fennel seeds and 2 drops essential oil of rose or rose geranium. Add the essential oil to the water immediately before you steam your face.

Aromatherapy to Relax or Recharge

The word *aroma,* meaning "a pleasant or agreeable odor arising from spices, plants, or flowers," combined with the word *therapy,* or "the remedial treatment of a disease or other physical or mental disorder," gives us the true definition of the word *aromatherapy:* a healing modality that involves the use of aromatic essences or essential oils of plants.

Incorporating essential oils into your life is a pleasurable way to enhance your physical, emotional, and spiritual well-being. Aromatherapy can beautify your complexion, reduce stress, stimulate creativity, lull you to sleep, and pep you up, as well as help heal severe burns and reduce scar formation.

Strike a Balance

One of the easiest and most pleasant ways to benefit from aromatherapy is in the bath. At day's end, add 3 to 6 drops of your favorite gentle essential oil, such as lavender, Roman or German chamomile, or clary sage, to a full tub of water and swish with your hands to blend. Slip into the water and breathe deeply. Relax ...

Intensify the potency of your peppermint tea. Give it a little zing by adding 1 or 2 drops of essential oil of peppermint. Inhale the invigorating steam. This tea is super for a midmorning pick-me-up, or to relieve a stuffy head or case of indigestion. Makes your breath minty-fresh, too!

To ease the pain of muscle cramps, sore tendons, arthritis, or overexertion in general, the clean, fresh, lemony scent of essential oil of eucalyptus citriodora makes a soothing addition to massage oil. Add 10 to 15 drops of essential oil to ½ cup of almond, hazelnut, grapeseed, or soybean oil, mix well, and massage away the discomfort. Enlist the help of a partner or good friend if possible, and promise to return the favor.

This formula can be adjusted to suit your particular emotional and physical needs. You may want to create all three versions so that you'll have the appropriate one on hand when you need it. **Caution:** *These formulas are for inhalation only. Do not apply directly to the skin; they may cause irritation.*

> 1 tablespoon pure, unrefined almond, jojoba, or hazelnut oil
> 1 of the following blends:
>
> **Calming Blend:** For excess stress, restlessness, or trouble sleeping, or if the weather outside is cold and dry, add ½ teaspoon lavender, ½ teaspoon neroli, ½ teaspoon clary sage, and ½ teaspoon bergamot essential oils.
>
> **Cooling Blend:** For times of irritability, impatience, fiery disposition, or chaos, or if the weather outside is hot and uncomfortable and your skin is extra sensitive and itchy, add ½ teaspoon lavender, ½ teaspoon jasmine, ½ teaspoon Roman chamomile, and ½ teaspoon spearmint essential oils.
>
> **Stimulating Blend:** If you're feeling slow and lethargic, in need of an energetic lift, and maybe a bit congested, or if the weather is dreary, cool, and damp, add ½ teaspoon cinnamon, ½ teaspoon orange, ½ teaspoon ginger, and ½ teaspoon cypress essential oils.

Combine the base oil with the blend of your choice in a 2-ounce, dark-colored glass bottle and cap tightly. The blend needs one week to synergize and develop, so shake your formula vigorously twice daily for seven days. After one week, place a few drops on a soft handkerchief or tissue and inhale the comforting herbal aroma as needed. The aroma can also be inhaled directly from the bottle.

Make a Splash

Nothing is more cooling and invigorating to hot summer skin than a chilled splash or spritz of a freshly made, fragrant natural skin toner. Like a summer breeze that soothes your parched skin and revives your senses, these lightly scented toners can be customized to your particular skin type and fragrance preference.

Give Your Skin a "Drink"

Natural skin toners have been used for centuries to refresh, pamper, and gently scent the skin and air. The following toner recipes can be applied as a splash, a light mist from a spray bottle, or with cotton balls. Use at any time of the day or immediately after cleansing to remove traces of cleanser and prepare your skin for moisturizer. Store in the refrigerator and discard after one week unless otherwise indicated.

For normal or oily skin, brew a cup of strong peppermint or lemon balm tea. Chill it, and use it to remove excess oil and shine from your skin.

For itchy, rashy skin, pour a cup of boiling water over 1 teaspoon of crushed fennel seeds. Steep for 10 minutes. Strain and chill.

For all skin types, brew a cup of strong chamomile tea, chill, and use to soften and moisturize. This is particularly good to use during the winter, when skin dehydrates and chaps easily.

For normal and dry skin, add 1 tablespoon of vegetable glycerin to ½ cup of rose water. The glycerin will act as a humectant and draw water vapor from the air to your skin. This makes a super, light floral summer moisturizer that can be stored in the refrigerator for up to six months. Shake before each use.

Polish Your Body

A cosmetic scrub is used to remove dry, dead cells from the surface of the skin. It can be used on all skin types except those with acne, thread (spider) veins, or extreme sensitivity; a scrub may be too irritating for such conditions. These recipes will leave your skin softer, sleeker, and more refined, in prime condition to absorb an application of moisturizer.

Natural Scrubs and Salt Rubs

For dry and/or sensitive skin: In a small bowl, combine 1 tablespoon of instant, powdered whole milk, 1 scant tablespoon of ground oatmeal, and enough water to form a spreadable paste. Allow to thicken for 1 minute. Massage onto your face and throat, avoiding the eye area. Rinse. This formula may be used daily in place of soap to gently cleanse your face and body. It will not irritate or dry your skin.

Especially for men or those with thick, oily skin: In a small bowl, combine 1 teaspoon of ground oatmeal, 1 teaspoon of finely ground almond meal, 1 teaspoon of fine sea salt, and ½ teaspoon of powdered peppermint or rosemary leaves with enough of your favorite herbal astringent to form a spreadable paste. Allow to thicken for 1 minute. Massage gently onto your face and throat, avoiding the eye area. Rinse. This blend is particularly good to use on the chest, back, or shoulders if minor pimple breakouts tend to occur.

For all skin types: In a small bowl, combine ¼ cup sea salt (or plain sugar) with ¼ cup of warmed coconut or olive oil. Stir together. Gently massage onto your body with your hands or a mitt using light but firm pressure. Continue massaging until a rosy glow appears. Rinse with warm water, then towel-dry. This blend is beneficial for those suffering from severely dry skin: It will effectively remove the top layer of dead skin cells, allowing for proper moisturizer absorption. *Note:* This scrub should not be used on your face or immediately after shaving any area of your body; it could cause stinging and irritation.

For all skin types, especially dehydrated: In a small bowl, combine 1 tablespoon of finely ground sunflower seed meal with 1 tablespoon of applesauce. Gently massage this paste onto your face and throat. Let it remain for 10 minutes so that the oils of the sunflower seeds can be released and absorbed into your thirsty skin. Rinse with warm water, and then pat dry.

GRINDING INGREDIENTS

In order to grind oatmeal, sunflower seeds, almonds, dried herbs, and similar ingredients, I like to use a regular coffee grinder specifically reserved for cosmetic making. A blender or food processor works well for batches larger than 1 cup. Either method will create a fine, powderlike consistency.

6

Step Lively

M y feet are killing me!" Do you ever say that at the end of a long day? Whether you're a construction worker, athlete, secretary, stay-at-home parent, or fashion model, your feet take a lot of abuse. Most people stuff their feet into ill-fitting shoes and suffer from cramped and strained arches, heel pain, hammer-toes, bunions, calluses, corns, and toe cramps.

If you want your feet to provide you with years of uninterrupted service, treat them with the utmost care. Daily hygiene and a few foot exercises go a long way toward this goal. Do keep in mind though, that 10 to 15 minutes of foot exercise every day will not do any good if you continue to wear ill-fitting shoes that constrict movement and force your feet into unnatural shapes.

Exercise Those "Dogs"

The following foot, ankle, and toe exercises can be performed anytime you feel the need to stretch and release tension. If you can't slip off your shoes discreetly during the day, then perform the exercises when you get home from work or finish your daily errands. Slip your body into something more comfortable and slip your feet out of something uncomfortable (your shoes). Relax and unwind. A nice cup of soothing herbal tea, sipped while you do your exercises, tastes especially good, hot or cold!

Footsie Roller Massage: Wooden footsie rollers have been around for many years. They come in all shapes and sizes, from single to double or triple rollers. Some are handheld, and others sit on the floor. I particularly like the kind with raised ridges going from one end to the other; these are both stimulating and relaxing to my feet. If you don't have a footsie roller, a wooden rolling pin can be used in a pinch. Simply place the footsie roller or rolling pin on the floor and, while bearing down comfortably, roll the entire length of your foot over the tool, back and forth. Repeat, concentrating on your arches. Do this for 5 to 10 minutes per foot. This exercise relieves fatigue and cramping, especially in your arches.

The Golf Ball Roll: This exercise is recommended by Carol Frey, M.D., director of the Orthopaedic Foot and Ankle Center in Manhattan Beach, California. "Roll a golf ball under the ball of your foot for 2 minutes. This is a great massage for the bottom of the foot and is recommended for people with plantar fasciitis (heel pain), arch strain, or foot cramps."

Point and Flex: This is a great exercise to stretch and strengthen just about everything from your knees down. Sit on the floor, legs stretched out in front of you and palms facing down at your sides. Now point your toes as hard as you can and hold for 5 seconds; then flex your foot up as hard as you can and hold for 5 seconds. Repeat a total of 10 times. If you experience cramping, cut back on your repetitions and gradually work up to 10.

Rubber-Band Big Toe Stretches: This exercise is helpful if you suffer from bunions or toe cramps resulting from wearing improperly fitting shoes. This exercise is also recommended by Dr. Carol Frey. Either sit on the floor with your legs stretched out in front of you and your palms on the floor beside or behind you, or sit in a chair with your feet flat on the floor. Place a nice, thick, moderately stiff rubber band around your big toes and pull your feet away from each other. Hold for 5 to 10 seconds, and then relax. Repeat 10 to 20 times. If this hurts, or if you have arthritis or bunions in advanced stages, do only as many as you can. Gradually increase as your toes gain strength.

7

Nourish Your Hair

Healthy, shiny, bouncy hair is a reflection of proper nourishment and a healthy lifestyle. Even if you use the highest-quality natural shampoos, conditioners, and styling aids, the condition of your hair will still suffer if your diet is lacking in necessary nutrients. If your hair seems lackluster, try modifying your diet.

How to Have Healthy Hair

Eat more protein if your locks are limp, lifeless, and slow growing. Good sources of protein include eggs, lean meats and fish, beans and seeds, whole grains, and low-fat dairy or soy products.

Get your ABCs. These vitamins are vital to the health of your hair and scalp. Good sources of vitamin A include cod liver oil; red, yellow, and orange vegetables and fruits; spirulina; egg yolks; and deep green leafy vegetables. Good sources of vitamin C include citrus fruits, deep green leafy vegetables, rose hips, tomatoes, berries, pineapple, apples, persimmons, cherries, bell and hot peppers, papayas, and currants. Good sources of vitamin B include lean beef, poultry, egg yolks, liver, milk, brewer's yeast, whole grains, alfalfa, nuts and seeds, soy products, deep green leafy vegetables, spirulina, wheat germ, molasses, peas, and beans.

Cut back on caffeine, alcohol, refined sugar and flour, and junky snacks. These empty-calorie foods deplete your body's stores of vitamins B and C.

Include iodine, sulfur, zinc, and silica in your diet. These four minerals are essential for proper hair health. Good sources of iodine include all types of fish, spirulina, sunflower seeds, iodized salt, and sea salt. Good sources of sulfur include turnips, dandelion greens, radishes, horseradish, string beans, onions, garlic, cabbage, celery, kale, watercress, fish, lean meats, eggs, and asparagus. Good sources of zinc include spirulina, barley grass, alfalfa, kelp, wheat germ, pumpkin seeds, whole grains, brewer's yeast, milk, eggs, oysters, nuts, and beans. Good sources of silica include horsetail, spirulina, nettles, dandelion root, alfalfa, kelp, flaxseeds, oat straw, barley grass, wheat grass, apples, berries, burdock roots, beets, onions, almonds, sunflower seeds, and grapes.

Rapunzel's Favorite Herb Tea

Now, I won't guarantee that this tea will make you sprout hair as long and lush as Rapunzel's, but this mineral-rich brew is a delightful way to nourish your hair from the inside out. This recipe uses dried herbs, and will yield 2 cups of tea.

> ½ teaspoon horsetail
> ½ teaspoon raspberry leaves
> ½ teaspoon nettles
> ½ teaspoon oat straw
> 1 teaspoon peppermint
> 2 cups boiling water
> Honey or lemon to taste (optional)

Add the herbs to the boiling water, then remove from heat. Cover and steep for 5 to 10 minutes. Strain. Add honey or lemon to taste, if desired. Sip slowly and enjoy!

8

Top 10 Healing Foods

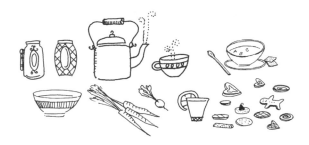

If you really want to pamper your mind and body, then partaking of these top 10 nutritionally dynamic foods is just what the doctor ordered. They'll help balance your moods; restore your energy; increase your stamina; nourish your hair, skin, and nails; and boost your immune system. They're delicious to boot!

Eat for Vibrant Health

Beans, beans, the magical food — the more you eat them, the better your mood! It's true: **Beans** are high in the B vitamins, known mood stabilizers. They're also high in complex carbohydrates, magnesium, iron, zinc, and fiber. A cup or so a day is recommended.

A cruciferous wonder, **broccoli** is a nutritional powerhouse. Just ½ cup several times per week delivers most of your daily required vitamin C, a dollop of vitamin A and the B complex, and plenty of minerals, especially calcium and magnesium; it's also rich in fiber.

The juicy, sweet **orange** is chock-full of skin-healthy, cold-fighting vitamin C, soluble and insoluble fiber, bioflavonoids, folate, and potassium. Consume one or more per day.

Apples are tasty, easy to carry, and thirst quenching. They're rich in soluble and insoluble fiber, potassium, and trace minerals. An apple a day sure won't hurt!

High in natural sugar, ripe **bananas** are self-contained packages of quick, healthy energy. They contain a fair amount of B-complex vitamins, vitamin C, and soluble and insoluble fibers, but are a good source of potassium and magnesium. Consume a few of these energy-boosting fruits each week.

Water can temporarily give you a feeling of fullness, hydrate your skin, keep your organs operating smoothly, and flush toxins out of your body. Drink 8 to 12, 8-ounce glasses each day, depending upon your level of activity.

Bone up on **sesame seeds.** These tiny, crunchy seeds are little storehouses of highly absorbable calcium and magnesium. They're also high in fiber and trace minerals. Look in health food stores for raw, unhulled seeds or jars of sesame tahini (sesame paste). Two tablespoons per day of seeds or paste will make a major contribution toward your daily mineral requirement.

Want a lean, low-calorie food that delivers a powerful nutritional punch? Then reach for **shell-fish.** Shrimp, scallops, clams, crab, abalone, lobster, snails, crayfish, oysters, conch, and prawns are high in beauty nutrients such as protein, B-complex vitamins, iron, iodine, zinc, and copper. Two servings per week are recommended.

Keep bacteria at bay and Dracula away by eating a clove or two of fresh **garlic** every day. This potent antioxidant can cut cholesterol, ward off infection, soothe a sore throat, protect your heart, and kill athlete's foot fungus. An ounce of fresh garlic contains a good helping of vitamin C, thiamin (vitamin B_1), potassium, sulfur, and iron.

Salmon is the king of flavor and a rich source of beneficial omega-3 fats, which have been determined to help prevent heart problems and lessen the symptoms of arthritis and PMS. One or more servings of salmon per week are recommended.

9

Five (Almost) Free Daily Rituals for Beautiful Skin

S kin care shouldn't be a complex chore. It should be simple, natural, and basic. And if a few of these straightforward skin-care rituals are free for the asking, then so much the better.

Tried-and-True Treatments

Cleansing Routine: A beauty must! Cleanse your skin twice daily (only once if your skin is dry) using a mild, natural, inexpensive cleanser designed for your skin type. Add a couple of drops essential oil of rose, spearmint, or orange to your cleanser to boost its cleaning effect and aromatic quality. Cleansing your skin is especially important before going to bed, because your body excretes toxins through your skin as you sleep. If facial pores are clogged with makeup and dirt, breakouts can occur. If you perspire a lot in your line of work or exercise heavily, then rinse off and massage your body with a coarse cloth or loofah before retiring to remove salt and dead-skin buildup. Your skin needs to breathe while you sleep!

Exercise: Try to exercise outside, to help oxygenate your cells with fresh air and facilitate waste removal through your skin. Exercises such as walking, biking, in-line skating, and weight lifting improve cardiovascular fitness and muscular endurance, which translates into increased energy and a rosy complexion. If you live in a city, try to find a green space — a park or a greenway — in which to exercise. If city streets, with their attendant pollution, are your only outdoor option, exercising in a gym may be a better alternative.

Sleep, **Blissful Sleep:** I don't care what else you do to your skin, if you are sleep deprived your skin will look sallow, dull, tired, and saggy; with your puffy eyes, you will resemble a frog prince or princess. And of course, your energy level will be less than desirable. Sleep: It's the best-kept skin-care secret there is!

Sunlight: Ten to 15 minutes unprotected exposure to sunlight several times a week is essential to the health of your bones and skin. It helps your body absorb calcium, due to the skin's ability to convert the sun's rays into vitamin D. Sun exposure helps heal eczema, psoriasis, and acne, and energizes your body. Plus those warm rays just make you feel good all over. If your dermatologist advises you to avoid the sun entirely, other sources of vitamin D include egg yolks, fish liver oil, vitamin-D-supplemented soy or cow's milk, organ meats, salmon, sardines, and herring.

Water: What goes in must go out, and water helps move everything along. Impurities not disposed of in a timely manner via the internal organs of elimination (such as the kidneys, liver, lungs, and large intestine) will find an alternate exit, namely your skin, sometimes referred to as the "third kidney." Pimples and rashes may develop as your body tries to unload its wastes through your skin. Eight to 12, 8-ounce glasses of pure water a day combined with a fibrous diet will help cleanse your body of toxins and keep your colon functioning as it should. Water also keeps your skin hydrated and moisturized, so drink up!

De-stress & Relax

Seems like everyone is so very busy these days, no matter what their job description. I've spoken with many stay-at-home parents, career men and women, elderly folks, and students, asking them for their favorite methods to relax and de-stress after a hectic day. Try some of these ways to unwind.

Take a Load Off

"If I am stressed, I like to go for a long walk, because it helps me unwind."

"If stressed while at work, I try to breathe in deeply and then exhale slowly."

"I find taking a leisurely bath with oils or a bubble bath to be very soothing."

"To relax, I like doing stretching exercises for about 15 minutes or so with my eyes closed while listening to calming background music."

"My greatest de-stressor is usually a creative pursuit. I make quilts and garden, primarily. The final products are lasting delights that I cherish."

"I have a monthly facial."

"Cooking relaxes my mind and body. Eating what I've prepared is great, too!"

"Sipping a glass of wine while reading a good book chases the day's cares away."

"Good heart-to-heart conversation, a romantic candlelight dinner, and a walk on the beach at sunset with my husband is my idea of heaven."

"I like to putter in my garden, feel the soil, and pull weeds after work."

It's High Time for Tea

Nothing's more relaxing and refreshing than a good cup of herbal tea. Tea herbs are easily grown in pots or in your garden; all it takes are good soil, a sunny spot, water, compost or fertilizer, and a bit of TLC. Herb seeds for tea gardens are available in most garden centers or through seed catalogs. Follow seed-package directions for proper sowing, care, and harvesting.

For Your Sipping Pleasure

Plant one or all of the following easy-to-grow herbal tea blends. See the directions that follow for brewing the ultimate cup of tea from your fresh herbs. *Note:* Please be sure to use only organically raised herbs for culinary purposes; you don't want to ingest pesticides.

Lemon Lover's Blend: 2 teaspoons each lemon balm leaves, lemon verbena leaves, and lemon-grass leaves, plus fresh lemon juice to taste.

Mad about Mint: 2 teaspoons each peppermint leaves, spearmint leaves, and lemon mint leaves.

Licorice Delight: 2 teaspoons each fennel seeds, anise hyssop leaves, and cinnamon basil leaves.

Tension Ease: 2 teaspoons each chamomile flowers, lemon basil leaves, and raspberry leaves.

Fresh-n-Fruity: 2 teaspoons each pineapple mint leaves, orange mint leaves, apple mint leaves, and ginger mint leaves.

Cup-o-Calmness: 2 teaspoons each catnip leaves, lavender blossoms and leaves, rose petals, and lemon balm leaves.

Tea is wealth itself, because there is nothing that cannot be lost, no problem that will not disappear, no burden that will not float away, between the first sip and the last.

— Henry David Thoreau

The Ultimate Cup-o-Tea

For many people, brewing the perfect cup of tea is akin to art. Whether or not you agree, you're sure to enjoy a delicious, soothing cup of tea whenever the urge strikes. To make iced tea, double the amount of herbs called for in the recipe and brew as usual. Chill in the refrigerator and serve over ice when ready.

> Several cups purified, cool water
> 2 tablespoons herbal blend of choice (see opposite)

1. Bring the water to a rolling boil. Add 2 cups of the boiling water to a pottery, china, or glass teapot, swirl around, and leave for a few minutes to warm the pot.

2. For each cup of tea, place 2 tablespoons or so of fresh herbs into a tea ball or strainer. Empty the warm water out of the pot. Toss in the herb-filled tea ball or strainer and pour in the desired amount of boiling water. Cover and steep for 5 to 10 minutes.

3. Remove the herbs and strain if necessary; serve. Nice additions include lemon or orange juice, honey, sorghum syrup, maple syrup, stevia syrup, date sugar, soy milk, and cream.

Soothe Your Soles

I f your nerves are frayed, your energy level is running on empty, and your feet have seen better days, then by all means partake of an aromatherapy foot massage. It will soothe your spirits, reduce stress, put the spring back into your step, and soften your feet. What's good for the body is good for the "sole"!

Techniques of Foot Massage

Here are some standard foot-massage techniques that a professional nail technician might perform on a client during a pedicure. If you do not have a willing partner to give you a massage, never fear. These techniques are just as easily done by you on your own feet. Foot massage can be performed on dry or slightly oiled feet, using any vegetable oil and a drop or two of your favorite essential oil.

Step 1: Stroking stimulates circulation and warms the foot. Holding your partner's foot in your hands, on the top of the foot begin a long, slow, firm stroking motion with your thumbs, starting at the tips of the toes and sliding back away from you, all the way to the ankle; then retrace your steps back to the toes with a lighter stroke. Repeat this step three to five times. Now firmly stroke the bottom of the foot with your thumbs, starting at the base of the toes and moving from the ball of the foot over the arch, to the heel, and then back again. Repeat this step three to five times.

Step 2: Ankle rotations will loosen the joints and relax the feet. Cup one hand under the heel, behind the ankle, to brace the foot and leg. Grasp the ball of the foot with the other hand and turn the foot slowly at the ankle three to five times in each direction. With repeated foot massages, any stiffness will begin to recede. This is a particularly good exercise for those suffering from arthritis.

Step 3: Toe pulls and squeezes can be unbelievably calming, because toes are quite sensitive. Grasp the foot beneath the arch. With the other hand and beginning with the big toe, hold the toe with your thumb on top and index finger beneath. Starting at the base of the toe, slowly and firmly pull the toe, sliding your fingers to the top and back to the base. Now repeat, but gently squeeze and roll the toe between your thumb and index finger, working your way to the tip and back to the base. Repeat on the remaining toes.

Step 4: Toe slides are also very soothing. Grasp the foot behind the ankle, cupping under the heel. With the index finger of the other hand, insert your finger between the toes, sliding it back and forth three to five times.

Step 5: The arch press releases tension in the inner and outer longitudinal arches. Hold the foot as you did in step 4. Using the heel of your other hand, push hard as you slide along the arch from the ball of the foot toward the heel and back again. Repeat five times. This part of the foot can stand a little extra exertion, but don't apply too much pressure.

Step 6: Stroking is a good way to begin and end a foot massage. Repeat step 1, on page 35.

The way to health is to have an aromatic bath and a scented massage every day.

— **Hippocrates**

13

Take a Luxurious Milk Bath

Why not use the skin-pampering benefits of milk by bathing in it instead of drinking it? Milk includes many components, such as proteins and fats, that are particularly good for soothing and moisturizing the skin.

Milk — for Softer, Sleeker Skin

To relieve itchy skin due to sunburn or poison ivy or oak irritation, add 1 cup of instant, powdered whole milk and 1 cup of baking soda to running bathwater. Step in and soak for 15 minutes.

Make a milk-bath bag. In a medium-size muslin drawstring bag or in a 12-inch square of doubled cheesecloth, place 1 cup of instant, powdered whole milk, ½ cup of borax, ¼ cup of ground lavender flowers, and ¼ cup of ground rose petals. Tie the ends together or wrap with an elastic band. Drop into the tub as it fills with water, step in, and rub the bag over your skin to soften and lightly scent.

To combat dry, super-sensitive skin or to bathe an infant's delicate skin, add 1 cup of instant, powdered whole milk, ¼ cup of finely ground raw almonds, pine nuts, walnuts, or pecans, and ¼ cup of marsh mallow root powder to a bath bag (see above). Drop into the tub as it fills with water, step in, and rub the bag over your skin.

Aromatherapeutic Milk Bath

Try this version of Cleopatra's famous bathing ritual and see if your skin doesn't feel softer and smoother.

- 1 cup instant, powdered whole goat's or cow's milk
- 1 tablespoon apricot kernel, jojoba, avocado, hazelnut, or extra-virgin olive oil
- 8 drops essential oil of German or Roman chamomile, lavender, rosemary, spearmint, or rose

Pour the powdered milk and oil together directly under running bathwater. Add the essential oil immediately before you step into the tub. Swish with your hands to mix. Now relax!

14

Cleanse & Condition Your Complexion

Simple, natural cleansing creams, fruit pastes, and grain blends can be used to effectively and economically remove makeup and everyday dirt and grime that collects in your pores. Unlike soap — which has a tendency to dry the skin's surface — these products are very gentle and nourishing and do a thorough job of cleansing without stripping your skin of its natural barrier of protective oils.

Restore the Radiance

For smooth, soft skin, wash your face every day with plain, organic yogurt or buttermilk. Use it as you would ordinary cold cream, avoiding the eye area. It's gentle enough for all skin types and as a bonus, it contains naturally occurring lactic acid. This acts as a mild exfoliant to remove dead-skin buildup.

For positively glowing skin, mash a third of a very, very ripe banana in a small bowl. Use the pulp to wash your face and throat, avoiding the eye area. If your skin is especially dry or dehydrated, leave this on for approximately 5 minutes. Rinse, then pat dry.

To pamper mature, thin, dry skin, mix 1 tablespoon of heavy cream with 1 or 2 drops of essential oil of rose or rose geranium. Use as you would a cleansing lotion, massaging well into your face and throat. This can be used on the eye area to remove eye makeup and mascara. This blend smells exquisite and if a drop happens to drip into your mouth, it will taste like a rose shake!

All-Purpose Cleanser

*This was my first-ever homemade cleansing formula —
created when I was 15! It's still my favorite recipe 21 years
later. It naturally cleanses skin of excess oils, makeup, and
dirt without drying, making it suitable for all skin types,
even sensitive. See the box on page 16 for information on
grinding ingredients.*

½ cup ground oatmeal
⅓ cup finely ground sunflower seeds
¼ cup finely ground almond meal
1 teaspoon powdered peppermint or rosemary
  leaves, rose petals, or lavender flowers
Dash cinnamon powder (optional)
Water, 1 or 2 percent milk, or heavy cream to moisten

1. In a medium-size bowl, mix the dry ingredients together
thoroughly.

2. Using approximately 2 teaspoons of scrub mixture for
your face and throat, or more for your body, add enough
water (for oily skin), milk (for normal skin), or heavy cream
(for dry skin) to form a spreadable paste. Allow to thicken
for 1 minute. Massage onto your face and throat or body
area. Rinse.

3. Store any remaining blend in a zipper-lock plastic bag or
plastic food container in a cool, dry place for up to six
months, or up to a year in the freezer.

15

Keep Your Pearly Whites Gleaming

Most dentifrices available today contain harsh abrasives, saccharin, sugar, detergents, and bleaches. Combine these ingredients with the twice-daily use and misuse of toothbrushes and the result is tooth enamel and gum tissue suffering from extra wear and tear. You can make simple yet effective and pleasant-tasting natural dentifrices at home that will leave your teeth sparkling and your gums in the pink.

Step Back, Plaque

In a small bowl, combine 1 teaspoon of baking soda with 1 drop of essential oil of orange, lime, spearmint, or cinnamon. Dip a wet toothbrush into this mixture and brush your teeth as usual to fight plaque buildup and neutralize mouth odor.

Try strawberries for a brighter smile! Mash a very ripe strawberry into a pulp. Dip your toothbrush into the pulpy liquid and brush normally. Strawberries have a slight bleaching action. Rinse thoroughly after brushing.

Out on a weekend camping trip and forgot your toothbrush? Peel a 3- or 4-inch twig freshly cut from a sweet gum or flowering dogwood tree and chew on the end until it is frayed and soft. Now gently rub your teeth and gums. The twig can also be dipped in water and baking soda, if you desire.

Herbal Toothpaste

A great alternative to commercial sweetened toothpastes!
This recipe yields about 10 applications.

- 4 teaspoons baking soda
- 1 teaspoon finely ground sea salt
- 1 teaspoon myrrh powder
- 1 teaspoon white cosmetic clay
- 2 tablespoons vegetable glycerin
- 10 drops essential oil of orange, tea tree, rosemary, anise, lemon, spearmint, or peppermint

In a small bowl, thoroughly blend all ingredients until a spreadable paste forms. Store in a small jar. Dip a dry toothbrush into the mixture and brush normally.

16

Find Time for Fitness

What's the first thing to go when your daily schedule gets overburdened? For most people, it's exercise. But exercise helps you deal effectively with the physical and psychological demands of a hectic life. How do you find more time or use the time you have more wisely to get healthy, toned, and trim?

Exercise Is Essential

Break up your exercise routine into 10-minute segments and try to fit three to six segments into your day. The benefits are practically the same as if you were to do just one long routine.

Find a better way to commute to work. If possible, walk or ride your bicycle. If that isn't possible, park a mile or two away from work and hoof it to the office. If you take a train or bus, get off at the stop prior to your regular one. Your legs will soon reflect all this added mileage!

Find creative ways to integrate family time with exercise. If you have children, don't just be a bystander at the local playground; get up and climb the jungle gym with them, or run around the bases playing softball. Push a jogging stroller and give Junior a fun ride. Try bicycling, hiking, swimming, or just walking around the neighborhood with your family. Everyone will be healthier as a result.

Schedule your exercise time. Make it a priority and stick to it just as you would a scheduled doctor's or dentist's appointment.

Work out first thing in the morning. I find that if I get my exercise finished and out of the way, I don't have to try to fit it in at the end of the day when I'm usually tired and might be tempted to skip my workout altogether.

Combine work with exercise. Sound strange? I love to in-line skate and while I'm whizzing up and down my neighborhood streets, I carry a small tape recorder and make notes as I skate. My neighbors thought I was a bit strange at first, but they're used to me now. You can do this as you walk, also.

Make dinner while you exercise. If you enjoy one-pot dinners or main-course casseroles, pop one on the stove or into the oven and do your workout while it cooks. A Crock-Pot is a real blessing for busy people. It cooks long and slow so you can do other things while making dinner. As a bonus, exercising before you eat may take the edge off your appetite — and boost your metabolism, too.

Make exercise time *your* time. Remember, there's no better way to pamper yourself than by taking care of your health.

Health is something we do for ourselves, not something that is done to us; a journey rather than a destination; a dynamic, holistic, and purposeful way of living.

— Dr. Elliott Dacher

High-Energy Snacks

In the mood for a snack? Need fast food that will satisfy your cravings yet not be filled with empty calories and fat? Well, look no farther. Here are a few of my favorite delicious, guilt-free, quick snacks.

Need a Boost?

For a super-cooling summertime snack, nothing beats sweet, frozen, seedless grapes. They're a tasty, crunchy treat that's full of vitamins and minerals.

Fight the midafternoon attack of the Munch Monster by eating one of my favorite snacks — medjool dates. Slice a large date in half, remove

the pit, insert a raw pecan into each half, then
sprinkle with coconut flakes.

To organic plain yogurt or fortified soy yogurt,
add any or all of the following: ripe raspberries,
blackberries, sliced peaches, strawberries, kiwi,
papaya, almond slivers, raisins, granola. Stir well
and drizzle with honey or maple syrup, if desired.

For a high-protein snack, top melba toast or a rice
cake with peanut or sesame butter or cottage cheese.

Sweet-n-Nutty Snack Mix

*Convenient and portable, this mix is 100 percent better
for you than a candy bar or chips! You'll get approximately
3½ cups from this recipe.*

  ½ cup raw almonds
  ½ cup raw hazelnuts
  ½ cup dried, unsulfured, pitted cherries
  ½ cup large, unsulfured raisins
  ½ cup raw Brazil nuts
  ¼ cup lightly salted sunflower seeds, toasted
  ¼ cup lightly salted pumpkin seeds, toasted
  ¼ cup dried, unsulfured apricots, chopped
  ¼ cup carob or chocolate chips (optional)
  Dash cinnamon or nutmeg (optional)

Place all ingredients in a plastic bag or food storage container and shake well. Keep tightly sealed in the refrigerator
unless consumed within two weeks; raw nuts become rancid
quicker than roasted ones. Consume a handful or so whenever the snacking mood strikes.

Harness the Power of Your Shower

Turn your ordinary daily cleansing shower into a therapeutic spa. While a tub full of warm, sudsy, aromatic water conjures thoughts of relaxation, a shower can offer a wide array of body-pampering benefits simply by concentrating the flow of water onto specific body parts, enabling you to tackle problems such as sore muscles, headache, low energy, and lackluster hair, to name a few.

Hydrotherapies

Increase Your Energy: Shower in water that's approximately body temperature for 2 to 3 minutes, then lower the temperature to very cool for about 15 to 30 seconds. Repeat this procedure twice more. Incidentally, this form of hydrotherapy has been used for centuries by many cultures to strengthen the immune system, thereby staving off colds and flus.

Hydrate Scaly Skin: For skin that resembles a desert reptile's, take a quickie shower for about 2 minutes in warm water. While your skin is still wet, slather on your favorite body oil, then pat dry.

Head Off a Headache: A handheld shower apparatus is best for this type of therapy. Turn on very warm water and aim the stream directly onto the aching area of your head for 5 minutes. Frequently, simply aiming the water onto the back of your head and neck will ease the pain. Some people find that alternating very warm and cold water every 30 seconds for 5 minutes works wonders, too.

Reduce Swelling: To reduce inflammation to an acute injury such as a burn, sprained ankle or wrist, or severely stubbed toe, aim a cold spray of water onto the affected part for 5 minutes, then off for 5 minutes, repeating a few times. Do this immediately after the injury occurs, then seek medical attention if necessary.

Relieve Sore Muscles: For muscles that are chronically sore or are sore from mere overexertion, but are not inflamed, aim a very warm water spray directly onto the muscle(s) for 5 minutes, then off for 5 minutes. Do this a few times.

Put an End to PMS Pain: To relieve lower-back pain occurring before and/or during menstruation, I find that a very warm stream of water concentrated on my lower back for a few minutes helps lessen the cramping and muscle tension. Follow with a rich moisturizer to avoid dry skin.

Condition Your Tresses

Most men and women today style their hair to some degree daily. Whether it's simply a quick blow-dry or a complex ritual of moussing, drying, using hot rollers, brushing, then topping it all off with hair spray, your hair takes a lot of abuse.

Consider, too, environmental stress. Sunshine, salt water, chlorine, cigarette smoke, pollution, and dry office air all take their toll — hair is not meant to take this kind of constant torture.

Restore Your Crowning Glory

The following recipes are quite simple to make and, with consistent use, will improve the condition of your hair and scalp.

To condition dry, brittle, damaged hair, mash a very ripe, large banana. Add a tablespoon each of heavy cream and honey and whisk together until smooth. Apply to dry hair from the roots to the ends, cover with a shower cap, and then wrap your head with a warm towel. Allow the mixture to remain on your hair for as long as possible — up to an hour. Rinse thoroughly with warm water, then shampoo as usual. If necessary, follow with a natural, detangling light conditioner.

Enhance the gloss of normal or dry hair with jojoba oil. Actually a plant wax, not an oil, this yellow substance closely resembles human sebum. It makes a superb scalp and hair conditioner. To 6 tablespoons of jojoba oil, add 1 teaspoon each of the following essential oils: rosemary, basil, lemon, and lavender. Store in a 4-ounce, dark glass bottle. Shake vigorously before each use. Use within one year for maximum potency. Apply 1 or 2 table-spoons to dry hair and scalp. There's no need to soak your hair; just make sure all the strands are coated thoroughly. Be sure to give your scalp a good 5-minute massage to stimulate circulation and encourage hair growth. Cover your head with a shower cap and wrap with a warm, damp towel for up to an hour. Shampoo and follow with a good, light detangling conditioner if necessary. This treatment may be used weekly.

Rinse, rinse, rinse. If smooth and silky hair is your aim, proper rinsing is crucial. Even the best conditioners will leave your hair drab and dull if not rinsed out completely.

Tressonaise

Smooth your mane with this recipe for homemade mayonnaise filled with hair-healthy conditioning ingredients that will add shine and softness.

>   1 whole egg plus 1 yolk (room temperature)
> 1½ tablespoons lemon juice
>   1 cup unrefined olive, avocado, or sesame oil

1. Break the eggs into the blender, add lemon juice, and blend on medium for about 5 seconds. Remove the center plastic stopper from the cover, turn the blender back on, and begin to drizzle the oil in a slow, steady stream until all the oil is used. The mayonnaise should now be nice and thick.

2. Scrape out the mayonnaise using a long, flexible spatula and store in a covered, glass container in the refrigerator. This recipe makes one treatment for long hair, two treatments for shoulder-length hair, or three treatments for short hair.

3. To dry hair, apply enough mayonnaise to cover the damaged parts. If you have an oily scalp but dry, frizzy, damaged ends, then treat only the lower portion of your hair. Cover your hair with a shower cap or plastic bag, then wrap with a warm towel. Allow to remain on your hair for up to an hour, then shampoo once or twice to remove all traces of oil. Follow with your usual conditioner if you need to detangle. You may use once a week, if desired.

20

Take the Sting Out of Sunburn

It happens every spring: One of those unseasonably warm days comes along to tease and tantalize and make you throw caution to the wind. You decide to toss on your skimpiest bathing suit, bare your sun-starved skin to the warm air, and soak up a few rays. A few hours later, you wake up from dreamland. You run inside, look in the mirror, and uh-oh, you look like a lobster — and it hurts!

It's essential to rehydrate your skin immediately following a burn to restore pH balance and soothe the tender, injured tissue.

Soothe That Sunburn

Refrigerate your creams and lotions during hot weather for a skin-chilling, sunburn-soothing treat!

Add 2 cups of apple cider vinegar to cool bathwater. Soak for 10 to 20 minutes.

Spray a chilled German chamomile or lavender aromatic hydrosol directly onto the sunburned area to reduce redness and inflammation.

Spread yogurt or sour cream on itchy, burning skin for quick, super-cool relief.

Apply cold, strong, black tea directly to sunburn with soaked cotton pads. Use several times per day.

Aloe After-Sun Relief Spray

For skin that's hot, itchy, red, tender, and possibly blistered, reduce the temperature by taking a cold bath or shower. Pat your skin dry, then generously spray on this formula. Store the spray in the refrigerator for up to six months.

    1 cup aloe vera juice (*not* gel)
   20 drops essential oil of lavender
   10 drops essential oil of calendula
   20 drops essential oil of carrot seed
    5 drops essential oil of peppermint or rosemary
      (optional, for cooling effect)

1. Place all ingredients in an 8-ounce, dark glass spray bottle and shake well. Spray on sensitive burned skin as often as necessary to help hydrate, soothe, and protect.

2. Follow the spray treatment with a good, thick, natural moisturizer to help restore pliability to your dried-out skin. Pat, don't rub or massage, into the sunburned skin

21

Anti-aging Secrets

The search for the ever-elusive Fountain of Youth is still going strong. This is evidenced by the scores of commercials advertising the sale of anti-wrinkle creams, skin-lightening creams, energy-boosting nutrition supplements, and memory-enhancing herbal products, not to mention the increasing popularity of plastic surgery.

The way I see it, true youthfulness can't be purchased in a bottle or from a doctor. But the attributes of youth — smooth skin, an alert mind, an active, limber body — can be prolonged into old age by adhering to a youthful lifestyle and using common sense.

Maintain a Youthful Lifestyle

The old adage, "Early to bed, early to rise, makes you healthy, wealthy, and wise," still rings true today. Getting plenty of quality, sound sleep allows your body to rest, recharge, repair, and replenish so you'll be rarin' to go the next day.

Stimulate your brain. Don't allow yourself to become bored with life. Pick up a new hobby, find a new challenge, go back to school, read more. You *can* teach an old "dog" new tricks!

Become a "people person." Reach out and try to help someone every day.

Slow down; pace yourself. Quit scurrying around like a squirrel preparing its nest for winter. You can't enjoy life if you run through it at breakneck speed.

Get a pet. Studies show that pet owners live healthier, happier, less stressful lives.

Hydrate your skin. Dry skin ages prematurely, exhibiting lines and wrinkles long before Mother Nature intended. Apply a good moisturizing lotion each morning and evening. Don't forget to consume eight glasses of pure water daily, too!

Wear sunscreen. Nothing ages your skin faster than exposure to the sun's rays. Sun damage is cumulative. That golden tan of youth will eventually produce unwelcome wrinkles, uneven pigmentation, age spots, and potentially skin cancer in your middle and later years.

Eat fresh, whole, unprocessed foods. Avoid empty-calorie, junky, chemical-laden foods. They do nothing but satisfy a temporary craving. Real food satisfies your soul and truly nourishes your body.

Exercise daily. Use it or lose it! A sedentary lifestyle contributes to obesity, cardiovascular problems, stiff joints, lackluster skin and hair, and low energy — all signs of old age.

Keep a positive attitude. Negativity not only affects your mood, your job performance, your physical appearance, and your health in general, but affects the people around you as well. No one wants to be around a person with low self-esteem.

Simplify your life. It's not the material things in life that bring true happiness, it's friends, family, good food, pets, and time spent doing things you most enjoy.

22

Stay Cool & Dry

Natural body and foot powders are a chemical-free way to fight odor and perspiration. You can easily make your own customized body powders that will keep you cool and dry all day long.

Herbal Body & Foot Powders

Some excellent base-powder choices to use alone or in combination include cornstarch, rice flour, arrowroot, French clay, white cosmetic clay, powdered calendula flowers, and powdered chamomile flowers. Customize your powder by adding your favorite essential oils or powdered flowers. Powders are simple to formulate and are great gifts.

My favorite mixture is 1 part cornstarch, 1 part arrowroot, and 1 part powdered calendula flow-

ers. This mixture makes for a very light powder
— perfect for infants.

To keep your feet cool, dry, and odor-free, try
this blend: Combine ½ cup of baking soda,
2 tablespoons of zinc oxide powder, 2 tablespoons
of white cosmetic clay, ½ cup of arrowroot, and
1 teaspoon of essential oil of orange, geranium, or
peppermint. If you have athlete's foot or particularly odoriferous feet, substitute ½ teaspoon each
of essential oil of tea tree and thyme. To make,
follow the directions in the recipe below. Sprinkle
into your shoes and socks once or twice daily.

For those with allergies, a powder made from
100 percent arrowroot powder, cornstarch, or
white cosmetic clay will generally be irritation-free.

Lavender Powder

*This is a delightfully soft, silky body powder. The recipe
makes about 1⅛ cups.*

- ½ cup white cosmetic clay, arrowroot, or cornstarch
- ¼ cup powdered lavender flowers
- ¼ cup powdered rose petals
- 1 tablespoon zinc oxide powder
- ½ teaspoon essential oil of lavender
- 10 drops essential oil of rose (optional)

Mix the dry ingredients in a large bowl or food processor.
Add the essential oils a few drops at a time and thoroughly
incorporate into the powder. Store this in a special shaker
container or recycled spice jar. Use within one year.

23

Cultivate Some
Zzzzzzzzzs

Has your get-up-and-go got up and gone? Suffering from brain fog? Too much on your mind to relax? Feeling constantly cranky? Insomnia a problem lately? Sleep deprivation takes its toll on both your face and body in a hurry. To look and feel your absolute best, you need to get approximately seven to nine hours of deeply restful, quality sleep each night.

"Perchance to Dream..."

Flannel sheets are an insomniac's best friend! Year-round, I sleep between thick, 6-ounce flannels that feel like light, soft, velvety blankets of fluffy cotton. During hot summer weather, forgo the usual thin blanket and substitute the top flannel sheet as your cover.

Get plenty of vigorous exercise early in the day so you'll be naturally tired come bedtime. Exercise performed too close to retiring can be too stimulating for some people.

Sip a cup of hot catnip, chamomile, or raspberry leaf herbal tea. Hot, mineral-rich vegetable broth, cow's milk, and calcium-fortified soy or rice milk are also good. Drink it an hour prior to bedtime or you'll wake up needing to visit the lavatory.

Don't go to bed on a full stomach. Digestion takes lots of energy and will keep you awake.

Go to bed at the same time every night. Once your body gets used to a routine, it will naturally want to fall asleep at that time.

Put a drop or two of soothing essential oil of lavender or Roman chamomile on your pillow.

Avoid caffeinated products such as certain brands of pain relievers, diet pills, and the usual culprits — coffee, cola drinks, chocolate, and black tea. Not only does caffeine keep you awake, but it also makes for more restless sleep and acts as a diuretic, causing you to make more trips to the bathroom.

Install light-blocking curtains or shades. These will help you stay asleep.

Purchase a device that drowns out disturbing noises and produces sleep-inducing sounds such as ocean waves lapping the shore, a gently babbling brook, or wind in the trees.

There must be stillness for the spirit to enter.

— **Anonymous**

Sleepytime Balm

So simple to make, yet so effective. Gentle enough to safely pacify even the most irritable, restless infant.

- ¼ cup all-vegetable shortening (room temperature)
- 10 drops essential oil of orange
- 2 drops essential oil of ylang-ylang
- 1 drop essential oil of vanilla (optional)

Combine all ingredients in a small bowl and whip together using a small spatula or whisk. Apply a dab of balm to your temples after cleansing your face and just prior to bedtime. Use daily, if desired. Store in a 2-ounce plastic or glass jar in a dry, cool place for up to three or four months.

Fortify Yourself against Cold & Flu

Feed a fever, starve a cold." Or is it "Feed a cold, starve a fever"? All I know is that when I'm achy, stuffy, and miserable, I want relief and I want it fast!

Commercial flu and cold medications always leave me feeling woozy or severely parch my sinuses and throat. They offer nothing in the way of health benefits, only temporary symptom relief.

After years of experimentation, I've finally hit upon two tried-and-true formulas that are guaranteed to return you to the land of the living in no time at all. They're nutritious and delicious ways to help your body heal itself without leaving you feeling like a blob!

Zesty Cider

A spicy, warming, tasty, natural antibiotic. This cider tastes good as a zippy salad dressing, too! Try to use organic ingredients. This recipe makes approximately 1½ quarts.

> 50 cloves garlic (not elephant garlic), minced
> 3 tablespoons dried or 6 tablespoons fresh echinacea root, grated or chopped
> ¾ cup fresh horseradish root, grated
> ½ cup fresh gingerroot, peeled and sliced
> 3 medium-size white onions, diced
> 1 teaspoon cayenne pepper powder or 3 fresh habañero peppers, diced and seeded
> Honey to sweeten, if desired
> 2 quarts raw apple cider vinegar

1. Place all ingredients in a 2-quart widemouthed jar. Fill to the top with vinegar. Cover the top of the jar with plastic wrap, then screw on the lid.

2. Refrigerate for six weeks so the flavor can develop and soften. Shake daily. There's no need to strain and bottle unless you want to. I think the flavor keeps getting better and bolder the longer the formula is allowed to steep.

3. At the first sign of a cold or flu, take 2 tablespoons of Zesty Cider with a warm water chaser. Rinse your mouth out well after swallowing the cider. Repeat once or twice daily for the duration of the illness. You should feel your sinus and bronchial passages quickly open and breathing become easier.

4. For a sore throat, gargle with the Zesty Cider straight for 60 seconds, spit, then rinse out your mouth. You should feel immediate relief.

Southwestern Chicken-Vegetable Soup

A very warming, spicy soup that serves up immune-boosting nutrition and opens sinus and bronchial passages, allowing for freer breathing. Try to use organic ingredients. This soup freezes well, and the recipe makes approximately 15 cups.

1	medium-size white onion, diced
20	cloves garlic (not elephant garlic), minced
2	celery stalks, sliced very thin
2	tablespoons extra-virgin olive oil
8	cups homemade chicken stock
3	carrots, sliced very thin or cubed
2	medium-size potatoes, cubed
1	tablespoon fresh lemon juice
½	teaspoon cayenne pepper powder or 1 habañero pepper, diced and seeded
1	tablespoon fresh parsley, minced
2	teaspoons fresh cilantro, minced
1	bay leaf
	Salt, pepper, oregano, savory, rosemary, or thyme to taste

In a 4-quart stock pot, sauté the onion, garlic, and celery in olive oil until transparent. Add the remaining ingredients and bring to a boil. Reduce the heat, and then cover and simmer for an hour. Eat a bowl whenever you feel the need for feasting and fortification.

25

Make Your Own Bath & Massage Oils

Bath and massage oils are very easy to make at home. You simply need a base oil and any essential oil you desire. I like to use jojoba oil as my base because it does not need refrigeration and will not go rancid. Grapeseed, apricot kernel, and hazelnut oils also make great base oils because they are very light, but they must be refrigerated.

Soften and Scent Your Skin

Uplifting, Energizing Oil: Combine 1 tablespoon of jojoba oil with 2 drops each of essential oils of peppermint, rosemary, and eucalyptus. Add to your bath while the tap is running. For a deodorizing foot treatment, have a friend massage your clean, tired feet with the oil for 15 minutes. Then put on socks, and go to bed.

Exotic Oil: This formula conditions dry skin and leaves a sensual, musky fragrance. Mix together ¾ cup jojoba oil with ¼ teaspoon each of these essential oils: sandalwood, patchouli, vetiver. Then add ¼ teaspoon of synthetic musk oil (optional). Store away from heat and light in a tightly sealed, 8-ounce, dark glass bottle. To use, add 2 teaspoons of oil to the bath while the tub is filling. For massage, use ½ teaspoon of essential oil blend to ½ cup of jojoba oil. For an exotic perfume, mix the essential oils only and bottle.

Nourishing Oil

This vitamin- and mineral-rich formula is good for all skin types, especially normal and dry. Excellent for dry, ragged cuticles, too.

1 tablespoon almond oil
1 tablespoon extra-virgin olive oil
1 tablespoon avocado oil
1 tablespoon jojoba oil
1 tablespoon apricot kernel oil
1 tablespoon hazelnut oil
1,200 international units (IUs) vitamin E oil (d-alpha tocopherol)

Combine all ingredients in an 8-ounce glass or plastic bottle. Tightly cap and shake vigorously. Store in the refrigerator for up to a year. For your bath, add 2 teaspoons to running water. For massage, use directly on your skin as needed.

26

Pamper Those Peepers

I t's said that the eyes are the windows to the soul. But if you look at a computer screen all day, party all night, spend time around smokers or in dry office air, have allergies, or forget to remove your mascara, your "windows" are going to look puffy, bloodshot, or irritated, or they'll have dark circles beneath them. They may even sting and tear.

Add Sparkle to Your Eyes

Your eyes are your most expressive features — do your best to pamper them. Follow these suggestions to soothe, brighten, and refresh red and weary eyes.

Pep up your pretty peepers with plenty of sound sleep — one of the best beautifiers there is!

Swollen eyes and dark circles can sometimes be the result of toxin buildup in the body, as well as dehydration. When the body is dehydrated, the kidneys try to retain water, which results in puffiness. Drink plenty of water daily in order to flush toxins and excess sodium from your body. The more water you drink, the less you will retain.

For swollen eyelids, dip cotton balls or cosmetic squares into icy-cold whole milk or cream. Lie down, and apply soaked cotton to your eyelids. Leave on for 5 to 10 minutes. The high fat content of either liquid provides a moisturizing treatment for the delicate, thin skin around your eyes.

Tune out. Don't be a TV addict. The glare from the screen is not good for your eyes. Besides, you can spend your time more wisely.

See your way clear by eliminating sore, dry, red, irritated eyes. My favorite treatment is to keep handy a bottle of lavender aromatic hydrosol and spritz my face and eyes with it as often as necessary. The liquid is so pure and gentle that I can spray it directly into my opened eyes. I find it extremely soothing. German chamomile and rose hydrosol work equally well.

Apply a chilled, water-based lotion or gel around the eye area once a day after cleansing to moisturize the delicate skin. A cucumber-based product is a good choice.

A daily application of sunscreen to the skin on and around your eyes is essential if you want to prevent sun damage and the formation of dark circles. Choose a product specifically designed to be used on the face.

Add 2 or 3 drops of essential oil of calendula to a small jar of chilled herbal eye cream. The resulting bright orange cream will help offset the blue color of dark circles, and the calendula essential oil is guaranteed to restore and soothe tired eyes, leaving them revived and refreshed.

Out of eye makeup remover? Apply a dab of all-vegetable shortening to the eye area and gently rub over your lashes. It will dissolve even the most stubborn waterproof mascara and eyeliner. Makes a great impromptu moisturizer for dry patches of eczema and psoriasis, too!

Give Yourself a Pedicure

W hat's the next best thing to a full-body massage? A professional pedicure. Take my word for it, the procedure is incredibly relaxing. If you can't fit a visit to your local nail technician into your budget or schedule, then you'll just have to pamper those tootsies yourself. A do-it-yourself pedicure will leave your feet fresh and supple, and you'll be in a better frame of mind, guaranteed!

Feet First

Set aside about an hour one evening per week to treat your feet. Surround yourself with all of the necessary supplies so you don't have to keep getting up and dripping water all over the house. Then follow these steps for smoother, more beautiful feet.

Step 1: The feet are one of the most receptive parts of the body, and a footbath is often just as relaxing or stimulating as a full-body bath. To your foot tub, add enough hot or cold water or herbal tea of your choice to cover your ankles, then a few drops of tea tree essential oil or a squirt of liquid soap or shower gel. Swish together. Soak your feet for 5 to 10 minutes to cleanse and soften calluses. Use this time to scrub your dirty toenails and soles using a toenail brush.

Step 2: After soaking, gently remove calluses with a pediwand, rasp, or stone. File down any corns with an emery board or diamond file.

Step 3: Dry your feet and legs when finished and remove any old, chipped nail polish using an oily, nonacetone nail polish remover.

Step 4: Time to exfoliate. Apply a mixture of 1 tablespoon each of salt and extra-virgin olive oil, plus 5 drops essential oil of peppermint to your feet and lower legs. Massage in circular motions concentrating on your heels, ankles, and any particularly rough, thickened areas. It will scrub off any leftover rough skin, and it feels and smells fantastic, too! Rinse your feet and legs. Dry with a coarse towel.

Step 5: Coax back cuticles with an orange stick and trim any that are ragged. Trim toenails straight across, rather than rounded at the corners, so that the white free edge is almost even with the top of the toe. File your toenails to smooth any jagged edges.

Step 6: Apply foot lotion, oil, or cream and massage in thoroughly for 2 or 3 minutes on each foot.

Step 7: If you're polishing your toenails, apply nail polish remover now to remove all traces of lotion or cream. Dry the nails. Now slick on a base coat, then two coats of your favorite color, followed by a top coat — allow each coat to dry in between. There's nothing like 10 freshly painted, glossy, perfectly pedicured toes to pick you up and make you feel pretty!

Step 8: After your polish dries, apply your favorite powder to your legs and feet, using a large puff or fluff brush to scent and prevent perspiration from taking a foothold.

28

Flower Power

The calendula flower, or pot marigold, is one flower you should familiarize yourself with. It's a beautiful, cheery, daisylike plant that is easy to grow in full sun and average soil; it can withstand heat, cold, drought, and even some dampness. This lovely, hardy flower has been used for centuries to gently and effectively heal many ills.

Rejuvenate and Heal

To heal minor cuts, scrapes, bee stings, and burns, apply calendula infused oil (see the recipe opposite) directly to the irritation.

For hard-to-heal dry, cracked skin, try calendula salve. For an instant salve, combine ¼ cup of room-temperature all-vegetable shortening with 20 drops essential oil of calendula. Stir well. Massage into affected parts as often as desired. This recipe also makes a soothing, gentle cream for diaper rash and ragged cuticles.

For an earache, place a few drops of warm calendula infused oil into each ear, plug with cotton balls, and leave overnight.

To brighten a salad, add fresh calendula blossoms along with violets and nasturtiums for a variety of tastes, textures, and colors.

Calendula Blossom Oil

You'll make about 4 cups of a potent healing oil that can be used as a salve base, massage oil, or bath oil. You can also use it in any healing formula calling for oil.

> 4–5 cups calendula blossoms, wilted for 24 hours in well-ventilated shade
> Extra-virgin olive oil

1. Put the calendula blossoms in a 3-quart pot and pour in enough olive oil to cover by 2 inches. Turn the burner on low. Heat the mixture to just below a simmer, and let it steep for 5 to 10 hours, uncovered. Check on it every hour or so to make sure the oil isn't simmering.

2. Remove from the heat after the oil smells herby and has attained a rich, golden-orange color. Cool, strain, bottle, label, and refrigerate. This oil will keep for six months to a year if refrigerated. Use within 60 days if not refrigerated.

29

Professional Pampering Tips

S elf-pampering is a wonderful way to address your emotional, physical, and spiritual needs, but sometimes it just plain feels better to put yourself into the hands of a professional. Here are some tips for a great pampering experience.

Day Spa Specialties

N ever had a full-body massage before? Then try a mini massage. Many day spas offer low-fee or even complimentary mini massages for your back, shoulders, or feet to entice prospective customers to sign up for a full treatment.

Next time you visit your hairstylist or barber, ask the shampoo technician to spend extra time performing a scalp massage. The tension will simply drain from your head. Make sure to tip him or her appropriately for a job well done.

Try an energy-balancing treatment such as reiki or polarity therapy. These noninvasive techniques can be used to facilitate all types of healing.

A spa manicure or pedicure is a change of pace from the usual variety. These can include a sea salt soak, a mud or paraffin mask, a full hand-and-foot reflexology treatment, followed by a softening peppermint cream massage. Ahhhh…

If you happen to be visiting a resort or hotel that offers mud baths, sign up! Warm, gooey, mineral-rich mud removes toxins from the skin and tones and tightens the pores. It's terrific for easing muscular and joint pain, too.

To soften, hydrate, and exfoliate your body, try a seaweed or herbal body wrap. These treatments are especially beneficial after a summer vacation in which your skin has been overexposed.

30

Brighten Your Home with Flowering Plants

I was born with a green thumb, inherited from my grandmother. It's a true blessing! Everything I touch seems to explode with bountiful growth and flowers. But fear not: Even if you're a certified "brown thumb," you can add brilliance, beauty, and fragrance to your home by cultivating these easy-to-grow varieties of plants.

The Power of Flowers

Nothing is prettier and more cheery than a room full of colorful flowering plants. Why not fill your home with blooms? One of the easiest plants to

grow is the Christmas cactus. If you have several
sunny windows in your home, buy a few plants in
red, white, salmon, pale pink, fuchsia, and the rare
golden-orange (if you can find it). Plant them in
clay pots, and you'll enjoy bountiful blooms from
Thanksgiving through Christmas and possibly
again around Easter. These plants require minimal
care, and like to be potbound.

Try your hand at forcing flowering bulbs —
causing bulbs to bloom out of season so that they
bloom inside your home in the dead of winter. In
the fall, visit your local nursery and pick up 5 to
10 hyacinth, paperwhite, daffodil, or tulip bulbs, a
relatively shallow pot especially for forcing bulbs,
and a small bag of white gravel, shells, or marbles.
Pour a layer of your chosen material about an inch
deep in the bottom of the pot; insert your bulbs
root-side down into the gravel, shells, or marbles;
then pour enough material around the bulbs to
reach about midbulb height. Fertilize with a liquid
flowering-plant fertilizer and keep the base of the
bulbs moist, not swimming in water, until flowering
is complete. Set pot in a bright, sunny window and
wait for blooming time.

If you receive a potted amaryllis bulb for
Christmas, be sure to save it, pot and all, after it
has finished blooming. Keep it indoors, barely
moist, until nighttime temperatures drop no lower
than 40° F, and then set it on your patio or steps

in partial sun for the remainder of the year. About early November, cut off all growth down to bulb-tip level, give it a good drink of liquid fertilizer, and put it in a sunny window. In a few months you'll have another round of blossoms, possibly more than the year before. Amaryllis bulbs grow larger each year, and the number of stems and blossoms increases as each bulb ages. These are large, showy flowers, growing about 1 to 2 feet tall, and available in a rainbow of colors.

Love the look of orchids, but afraid they might be hard to grow? Consult your local nursery about the how-tos of orchid growing and soon you'll have these delicate yet long-blooming beau-ties throughout your home. They're actually quite easy to grow provided your home temperature doesn't drop below 55° F in the winter. The com-mon phalaenopsis orchid blooms for about four months, comes in a variety of colors and sizes, and is simply glorious!

Buy a book on flowering houseplants and read up on proper care instructions for your newly acquired beauties. Some of my plants are so big now that I can't get them out of the house; they've outgrown the door width! Learn how, when, and with what to fertilize your plants, how much water and light they need, and when to transplant them for optimum health and growth.

Have a Honey of a Day

Honey — that sweet, thick, golden syrup produced by thousands of honeybees — not only tastes great on food but, as the Native Americans discovered, can also help heal myriad ailments, nourish your body, and soften your skin. Who would have thought that an everyday food could have so many uses?

Life Is Sweet

Cut your finger or scrape your knee? Put a few drops of honey on the affected area. Honey has been proven to be just as effective in most cases as standard topical antibacterial ointments and helps keep the cut or abrasion sterile and the surrounding skin soft so scarring is minimized.

Suffering from dry, finely lined skin? Try a "honey tap" facial. Moisten the skin, then apply a very thin layer of honey onto your face and neck (make sure to put your hair up first or things could get sticky) by tapping your honey-laden fingertips over your skin. The tapping revs up circulation, and the honey acts as a humectant to draw moisture to your skin. Lie down for about 15 minutes, then rinse with warm water. Your skin should be rosy, warm, moist, and glowing.

For nursing mothers, try massaging a dab of honey on dry, cracked, sore nipples. This is reported to soften the skin and aid in healing. Just make sure to rinse off the honey before nursing again, as infants under 12 months of age should not consume honey.

HEALING HONEY TIP

Use only unprocessed honey for topical use. It's available from health-food stores or from an apiary. It's not the same as the usual grocery-store varieties, which have been heated and filtered, rendering the beneficial enzymes and nutrients cooked and lifeless.

Soothe a sore throat by gargling with a cup of warm sage-honey tea. To a cup of boiling water, add 1 teaspoon dried sage. Steep for 5 minutes, and then strain. Add 1 tablespoon honey and stir. Gargle for 60 seconds as often as needed throughout the day; spit out the liquid. Rinse your mouth with water after each use so the natural sugars don't remain on your teeth.

Sweet Energy

This pick-me-up drink is chock-full of potassium, a natural energizer, in addition to B vitamins, fructose, glucose, and trace minerals. It is quite refreshing and invigorating, and can be drunk twice daily, especially when you're tired, achy, or suffering from stiff joints. This formula is reported to relieve the pain and inflammation of arthritis if consumed daily.

    2 teaspoons raw, unheated, unfiltered apple cider
      vinegar (available in health-food stores)
    1 teaspoon raw honey
  6–8 ounces water

Stir ingredients thoroughly in a glass and drink on an empty stomach. You can also use this liquid as a facial splash for sunburned, dehydrated skin.

32

Keep Your Skin in Super Shape

Professional estheticians (skin-care specialists) agree that there are certain basic procedures and rituals you must follow to ensure a lifetime of beautiful skin. Caring for your skin shouldn't be a chore, nor should it cost a fortune. Follow these simple tips recommended by my fellow esthetician friends for skin that is plump, soft, rosy, and glowing with vitality.

Esthetic Essentials

Try to have a professional facial at least twice a year.

Keep a mister bottle of either purified water or herbal aromatic hydrosol (available in health-food stores) handy at all times to refresh and hydrate your skin whenever you start to feel dry. This is especially important if you're a frequent flier.

Drink, drink, drink ... at least eight glasses of purified water every day.

Use sunscreen daily with a sun protection factor (SPF) of at least 15.

Cleanse, tone, and moisturize twice a day with products specifically created for your skin type. As you get older, reevaluate your skin type. Everything changes with age!

Eat a healthy diet and get plenty of outdoor exercise.

Learn to manage the stress in your life. Stress wreaks havoc on even the most beautiful skin.

Not only does beauty fade, but it leaves a record upon the face as to what became of it.

— Elbert Hubbard

33

Strengthen Your Fingernails

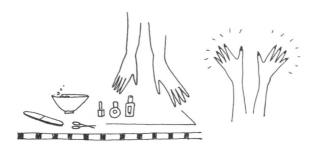

Beautiful, strong fingernails are generally a sign of good health and good habits. Your fingernails can become weak and brittle for a variety of reasons, such as lack of moisture, exposure to the elements or harsh household cleansers, or simply lack of proper care. See Nourish Your Nails, page 112 for more tips.

No-Nonsense Nail Care

Massage cuticles with a good, thick moisturizer or a dab of castor oil or vitamin E before bedtime.

Don't use your fingernails as tools. Instead, use a paper clip, screwdriver, or knife tip to pry something open or scrape off old candle wax or tape.

Don't cut your cuticles. Healthy cuticles contribute to healthy nails. Instead, gently push back oiled or moisturized cuticles with an orange stick wrapped with a small piece of flannel or soft cloth.

File your nails in one direction only; don't saw back and forth. Professional manicurists recommend using a diamond-dust or ceramic file to shape nails to a nice blunt oval.

Steer clear of fake nails. Research has shown that the chemical ingredients used for artificial nails and glue weaken the natural nail. There is also the potential for harmful fungus and bacteria accumulation.

Castor Oil Soak

This formula is good for dry, brittle, weak nails and cuticles. It takes just minutes to make and doubles as a terrific massage oil for dry hands.

> 4–5 tablespoons (60–75 ml) castor oil
> 10 drops essential oil of carrot seed or frankincense
> Contents of a small vitamin E capsule

In a small bowl, combine the oils. Soak clean fingertips for 5 to 10 minutes. Using a soft cloth, push back your cuticles and lightly buff your nails. You can use the same mixture for three treatments if it's kept covered and refrigerated.

34

Freshen Your Breath

Most commercial mouthwashes only serve to temporarily mask mouth odors, and contain artificial dyes, synthetic flavors, and harsh chemicals. Don't just cover up the odor, get rid of it by eliminating the cause of the problem.

No Offense!

For an antiseptic mouthwash and gargle, add 3 or 4 drops of essential oil of clove to 4 ounces of water. Swish in your mouth and gargle.

For breath that's tingly and spicy-sweet, suck on a dried clove or two.

Charcoal is a time-tested ingredient used to absorb poisons from the stomach, relieve gas pains, help treat diarrhea, and act as a breath purifier. Buy charcoal capsules; follow label directions.

Pyorrhea, or infected gums, can produce an unpleasant taste and odor in the mouth and should be seen by a dentist. In conjunction with your dentist's recommendations, dip a cotton swab into myrrh tincture and apply directly to sore gums and loose teeth.

Fight bad breath, clean your teeth, and stimulate your gums at the same time by using dental floss impregnated with essential oil of tea tree (available in better health-food stores). It is highly antibacterial and helps neutralize strong mouth odor.

After eating an especially garlicky meal, thoroughly chew a sprig of parsley and drink a cup of strong peppermint tea. Both herbs freshen your breath and also act as digestive aids.

For a super-effective antibacterial breath spray, combine ¼ cup each of distilled water and vodka, plus 5 drops each of essential oils of clove, anise, cinnamon, and orange. Store in a 4-ounce, dark glass bottle with a mister top. Shake before each use.

35

Protect Your Skin from the Sun

Light to moderate exposure to the sun makes us feel good, helps the body manu-facture vitamin D, gives us energy, and leaves a rosy-golden glow upon the skin. On the flipside, overexposure dries our skin, causing wrinkles, blotchiness, and premature aging. Sun protection is a hot topic these days.

Sun-Savvy Tips

In my opinion, 10 to 20 minutes of sun exposure several days a week, sans sunscreen, before 10:30 A.M. or after 4:30 P.M., is good for your physical health as well as your emotional well-being. However, if you are going to be in the sun for a longer period of time, by all means apply a sunscreen with an SPF of at least 15. Make sure the label indicates that the product provides UVA and UVB broad-spectrum protection.

Sensitive to chemical sunscreens? Try the titanium-dioxide-based products. Titanium dioxide is a natural mineral that acts as a physical block to UVA and UVB rays.

Remember the thick white stuff lifeguards used to put on their noses? That old standby, white zinc oxide cream, is still available, but now it's also offered in colors, which children really love. This cream totally blocks the sun. If you need every bit of protection possible, use zinc oxide cream on sunburn-prone areas such as your lips (be careful not to ingest), nose, ears, and shoulders.

There is no safe tan! Applying a topical vitamin C cream with a sunblock increases its effectiveness against skin damage, dehydration, and wrinkles.

The sun parches your skin, sucking it dry, so try to find a moisturizing sunscreen or apply your sunscreen first, allow it to dry, then apply a moisturizer on top of it.

PAYING A HIGH PRICE

In the July 1998 issue of *Elle* magazine, dermatologist Dr. Patricia Wexler stated, "More than 90 percent of the damage we see in aging is due to sun exposure. The sun damage you get today will show up twenty years later in terms of wrinkles, large pores, loss of elasticity, uneven pigmentation, precancerous cells, age spots, and skin cancer .... It's never too late to start with sunblock, but you shouldn't keep stalling."

Sunscreen Body Oil

This formula is good for normal and dry skin, medium or dark skin, or when minimal to moderate sunscreen protection is desired. **Caution:** *If you are fair skinned, you will likely need more protection. This recipe makes approximately 1⅛ cups of body oil.*

¼ cup anhydrous lanolin
¼ cup unrefined sesame oil
4 teaspoons vitamin E oil
¼ cup jojoba oil
⅓ cup aloe vera juice (*not* gel)
15 drops essential oil of bitter almond or patchouli,
    or 2–3 drops coconut fragrance oil

Combine all ingredients in one or two plastic squeeze bottles. Shake thoroughly before application. Reapply after swimming. Between uses, store the bottle(s) in the refrigerator. Use unrefrigerated oil within three weeks or discard.

36

If It Feels Good, Do It

When you were a child, did you run barefoot in the newly mown lawn just because it felt cool and wet and because you liked having green feet? Did you play in a warm summer rain shower just because it smelled fresh and felt so good on your hot skin? Did you go down to the local creek and stomp around in the gooey mud and let it squish between your toes just because it was there?

As adults, many of us have gotten stodgy and set in our ways. We've forgotten that life can actually be fun and silly and full of feel-good things. For once, just try being a child again. Do something out of the ordinary — just because you can!

What Should I Do?

Sing all day long — children do.

Skip everywhere you go. Feel like a child all over again.

Give your feet a vacation. If possible, don't wear shoes for a week, or just wear simple rubber flip-flops.

Take a walk in the rain and don't worry about what the neighbors will think when they see your hair dripping wet. As an added bonus, your hair will feel as soft as cat fur when it dries, and be nicely conditioned, too.

Take a hike in the woods when it's snowing. Notice how fresh and clean the air smells and how quiet and still it is.

How lush and lusty the grass looks! How green!

— William Shakespeare

Have a big glass of chocolate cow's milk or soy milk with breakfast. How long has it been since you enjoyed this yummy drink?

Buy a butterfly net and gently catch, identify, and release these delicate, beautiful creatures.

Collect colorful seashells on the beach. Fill an inexpensive, clear glass lamp base with the shells. You'll be reminded of your fun day at the beach every time you turn on that lamp.

If you have a garden, forgo the shoes for one day and feel the warm, soft earth caress your feet. If a rain shower happens to pass over, keep gardening. Enjoy the different scents, textures of the leaves, and insect life around you. It's amazing how vibrant you feel while communing this closely with Mother Nature.

If you have a dog or are friendly with a neighbor's dog, don't just simply pat him on the head; bend down and give him a bear hug. Ever notice what children do when they see a big, friendly dog? If they're not afraid of animals, they'll run right up to him and give him a great big full-body hug. He'll love the attention and so will you, in return.

37

Here's Zucchini on Your Face!

...**A**nd mint, and sage, and raspberries, and apples. Did you know that these common foods can do double duty by nourishing your insides and beautifying your outsides?

Beauty from Your Garden

Try these blends for five days of quick, fresh-picked skin-pampering treatments.

Day 1: Magic Mint Mask. This recipe sloughs off dead skin cells, absorbs excess oil, and makes your pores appear smaller. You'll need about 10

large peppermint leaves, ⅓ cup of water, and 1 tablespoon of white cosmetic clay. Add the peppermint leaves and water to a blender and mix until green and frothy. Strain. In a small bowl, add mint liquid to the clay and stir until a spreadable paste forms. Spread onto a clean face and throat and let dry. Rinse.

Day 2: Zucchini Zit Zapper. This mask is alkaline, soothing, and chock-full of skin-healing minerals. It is good for inflamed, sensitive, oily, or acne-prone skin. Blend 1 baby zucchini, 3 or 4 inches long, with ¼ cup of water in your blender until smooth and pale green. Strain. In a coffee grinder or dry blender, grind 5 tablespoons of oatmeal until coarsely powdered (see the box on page 16). Save some of this powder for day 4. In a small bowl, mix sufficient zucchini liquid with 1 to 2 tablespoons of powdered oatmeal and let thicken for 1 minute. Spread this paste on your face and throat and allow to dry for 20 to 30 minutes. Rinse.

Day 3: Raspberry Fruit Acid Slougher. You may be tempted to drink this recipe rather than put it on your face! The natural fruit acids gently remove the outer layer of dead skin cells. The mixture may sting raw, sensitive, or sunburned skin; rinse off immediately if this occurs. Puree ⅓ cup of fresh, ripe raspberries in your blender or small food processor with a tablespoon of heavy cream, or mash together using a mortar and pestle. Apply this liquid with cotton ball to already-cleansed skin and leave on for 5 to 10 minutes. Rinse, then pat dry.

Day 4: Apple Juice and Red Wine Purification Pack. This recipe acts as a natural fruit acid skin slougher and pore refiner and helps to gradually even out your skin tone. Juice 1 fresh, small apple. If no fresh juice is available, chop the apple and put it in a blender with ¼ cup of water and puree; strain. In a small bowl, mix 2 teaspoons of fresh apple juice with 2 teaspoons of red wine and 1 scant tablespoon of ground oatmeal (see day 2) to make a spreadable paste. Add more liquid if necessary. Smooth onto a clean face and throat and let dry for 20 to 30 minutes. Rinse.

Day 5: Sage or Chamomile Softening Hair and Body Rinse. A multipurpose product! You'll need ½ cup of tightly packed and chopped fresh sage or whole chamomile flowers (sage for brunettes, chamomile for blondes and redheads), and 1 teaspoon of borax. Add these ingredients to a medium-size saucepan and pour in 6 cups of boiling water. Cover and steep for 15 minutes. Now add ½ cup of apple cider vinegar. Strain and cool. Use 1 cup as a final rinse after shampooing to soften and add sheen to your hair. Refrigerate leftovers for up to 10 days.

38

Hand Therapy

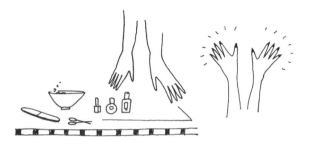

W̲e tend to pay so much attention to our faces and hair but neglect one of our most expressive features, our hands. They are constantly exposed to the elements — sun, wind, heat, cold, harsh cleansers, dirt, grease — and are one of the first places on our bodies to show age.

Basic Hand Care

A̲pply moisturizer frequently throughout the day, especially after contact with water.

W̲ear rubber or latex gloves when exposed to water or cleansers, and wear quality cotton gardening gloves when working outdoors. Waterproof, cloth-lined gardening gloves are recommended when working with moist or soggy soil.

Get in the habit of applying a moisturizing sunscreen with a sun protection factor (SPF) of at least 15. Sun damage can result in premature aging of the skin, blotchiness, dryness, and the development of those dreaded "liver spots."

Banish onion, garlic, and tobacco odors from your hands by rubbing them with diluted lemon juice or apple cider vinegar. Or place a couple of drops of essential oil of orange on your palms and rub your hands together vigorously. Rinse with cool water and follow with an application of moisturizer.

To exfoliate dry skin from your hands, try this simple formula: In a small bowl, combine 1 tablespoon of sugar with 1 tablespoon of olive oil. Stir well. Now massage your hands thoroughly, especially around the cuticles and in between your fingers in the webbing. Rinse thoroughly and apply moisturizer.

To hydrate parched hands, apply to them a layer of moisturizing facial mask. Follow label directions for application and removal.

39

Improve Your Rear View

If you're one of the few people who isn't afflicted with the lumps and bumps of cellulite, you're either very young or you've inherited one terrific set of genes. However, if you do have cellulite, there are several lifestyle "adjustments" you can make that will not only keep you healthier in general but also help prevent the formation or further development of cellulite.

Cellulite Treatment Tips

Get up, move, and sweat! Daily, vigorous aerobic exercise is paramount, so fight your sedentary tendencies. Try jogging, walking, dancing, bicycling, or in-line skating to stimulate circulation throughout your body, especially from the waist down (the area most commonly affected by cellulite).

Begin a regular aerobic weight-lifting routine to keep your underlying muscles toned and tight. It makes me really sweat and seems to carve the fat right off my thighs and buttocks as fast as a hot knife through butter. When I'm consistent about getting this type of exercise, I usually see results in as little as 10 days. Unfortunately, very few work-out tapes offer this type of exercise combination. Call your local gym to see if it offers classes.

Drink plenty of water. An ample intake of water will keep the toxins flowing right out of your body.

Eat a proper, balanced diet with as many whole, unrefined foods as possible. Reduce your consumption of refined and simple carbohydrates, including white flour, sugar and sugar substitutes, chips, cake, cookies, crackers, popcorn, and french fries, to name a few. Such starchy, sugary foods can cause weight gain and water retention.

Avoid salty foods like the plague! Salt causes your body to retain water, which can result in skin that looks puffy and bloated. This exacerbates the appearance of cellulite.

By all means stop smoking and avoid smoke-filled rooms. Smoking impairs circulation and adds poisonous toxins to your bloodstream.

Try yoga. If you've never taken a yoga-for-strength class, you may think that yoga is for people who can't do strenuous exercise. That assumption couldn't be farther from the truth. Yoga consists of performing a series of postures that strengthen your muscles and joints using your own body weight for resistance. I find that yoga tones and elongates my muscles, making for a leaner, more lithe look. It builds balance, coordination, and strength, and it's wonderfully de-stressing as well.

Dry-brush your skin every day. This is a wonderful technique for improving skin tone, circulation, and lymph flow, and for shedding dry skin. See Give Your Body the Brush-Off on page 109 for how-to instructions.

Keep alcohol and caffeine consumption to a minimum. They contribute more toxins for your body to deal with, and they sap your body of the nutrients essential for skin health.

Stay within your healthy weight range. Cellulite is more pronounced if you are overweight.

Eat for a Healthy Glow

For a dreamy, creamy, clear complexion, proper nutrition is essential. Our skin needs many different nutrients to maintain a healthy pH balance and glowing appearance. The two recipes that follow are chock-full of easily absorbable vitamins and minerals. They'll also provide you with a delicious way to boost your energy levels as well as your natural immunity.

Skin-Sational Herb Tea

A tasty blend for an infusion that, hot or cold, helps replenish a deficient system and restore lackluster skin. All the herbs in this formula are in dried form. You'll get 25 to 30 cups of tea from this recipe.

- 2 tablespoons lemon balm leaves
- 1 tablespoon lavender flowers
- 1 tablespoon peppermint leaves
- 1 tablespoon chamomile flowers
- 1 tablespoon rose petals
- 1 tablespoon nettles
- 1 tablespoon alfalfa
- 1 tablespoon rose hips
- 2 teaspoons dandelion leaves
- 2 teaspoons raspberry leaves
- ½ teaspoon gingerroot

1. Combine all herbs in a medium-size bowl and stir to blend. Store in a tightly sealed tin, jar, or plastic tub or bag in a cool, dark location. Best if used within six months.

2. To use, bring a cup of water to a boil in a small saucepan. Remove from the heat and add 1 teaspoon of tea. Cover and allow to steep for 10 to 15 minutes.

3. Strain before drinking. Add honey or lemon if desired. You can consume up to three mugs daily.

Earth laughs in flowers.
— Ralph Waldo Emerson

Skin So Smoothie

I refer to this recipe as my "antistress breakfast boost" formula. It's loaded with complexion-enhancing, stress-reducing B vitamins, calcium, potassium, zinc, iron, fiber, protein, and complex carbohydrates for sustained energy. I love the taste, but if you're not crazy about brewer's yeast, the flavor will take a bit of getting used to. This formula makes enough for approximately two 1½-cup servings or one large meal.

    1 frozen banana or 1 cup frozen strawberries
    2 cups organic low-fat cow's milk or fortified
       soy milk
    1 tablespoon brewer's yeast
    2 teaspoons blackstrap molasses
    2 teaspoons raw sunflower seeds
    1 teaspoon raw sesame seeds
   10 raw almonds
    ¼ cup raw or cooked oatmeal
    2 teaspoons honey
    ¼ teaspoon ground cinnamon
  2–3 ice cubes (optional; makes a nice thick,
       frosty drink)

Combine all ingredients in a blender and mix on high until smooth, 30 to 60 seconds total. I usually consume the entire batch throughout the morning hours, taking sips between my work projects. You can also pour half of the mixture into a mug, cover, and refrigerate until later in the day.

Give Your Body the Brush-Off

D ry, flaky skin is not only unsightly but uncomfortable, too. To eradicate dry skin, I recommend that both men and women adopt a simple yet invigorating morning ritual: dry-brushing, for epidermal stimulation. Dry-brushing revs up the circulation better than your morning cup-o-Joe, guaranteed. Perfect for those of you who suffer from winter "snake" skin.

Get Smooth and Healthy

Dry-brushing is a must for smooth, sleek, clear skin. Over the course of a day, your skin eliminates more than a pound of waste through thousands of tiny sweat glands. In fact, about one-third of all the body's impurities are excreted in this way.

If your pores are clogged by tight-fitting clothes, aluminum-containing antiperspirants, and mineral-oil-based moisturizers, there's no way for these toxic by-products to escape. Over time, the wastes build up, causing your skin to look pale, pasty, and pimply. The dead skin cells also build up on the epidermis, resulting in a dry, flaky, lizardlike texture that serves as a barrier impenetrable to most moisturizers. Ever keep applying moisturizer over and over again to your legs and arms yet still have that parched feeling, even though the bottle promises to alleviate even the most severely rough, dry skin? You have to get rid of the dead-cell buildup before the moisturizer can do any good! This is where dry-brushing lends a helping hand.

Contrary to what you might imagine, you can dry-brush over eczema and psoriasis. Granted, you may have to lighten up on your pressure a bit, but the stimulation is superb for those thickened, scaly, rough patches.

Repeat this ritual daily. It's a good idea to wash your body brush with soap and water every week or so to keep it free of skin debris.

Step 1: Dry-brushing is performed on dry skin — not oiled, not damp, but dry, before-you-bathe-or-shower skin. Using a natural-fiber brush the size of your palm, preferably one with a handle or strap, brush your entire body, except your face (and breasts, if you're a woman), for 5 to 10 minutes. Do not brush hard. Initially, you will have to start very gently and work your way up to more vigorous brushing, but never scrub until you're red. Begin brushing your hands first, between the fingers, then the arms, underarms, neck, chest, stomach, sides, and back. Then brush each leg, beginning with the feet. You will feel wonderfully invigorated when you're finished, and your skin will glow!

Step 2: Now pour a tablespoon or so of sesame, almond, olive, or avocado oil into a small bowl and add a drop or two of lemongrass, basil, German chamomile, or lavender essential oil. Massage your entire body, including your face, ears, and scalp if you're washing your hair that day. Do this for about 5 minutes. Next, jump in the shower and bathe as normal; all of the dead skin you just exfoliated will be washed away. Be sure to pat, not rub, your skin dry, and apply a light moisturizer after you shower if necessary.

A DRY-BRUSH BONUS

Here's an added plus to dry-brushing: Because the process opens your clogged pores and aids in elimination, your cellulite will begin to diminish. Trust me; it works. Follow a good, low-fat diet and exercise program, and it will work even faster.

42

Nourish Your Nails

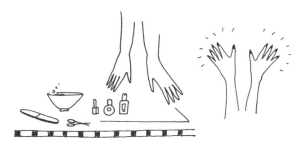

Nail problems that persist despite your consistent care can be a signal that something is lacking in your body. While some changes in appearance can be due to aging and climate, you should monitor your nails for signs of deeper problems. Your fingernails can suffer from brittleness, peeling, hangnails, weakness, ridges, discoloration, and spots if not fed the right foods. See your doctor if problems continue.

Fingernail Food

Nails are primarily composed of protein called keratin. Good sources of this essential nutrient include soy products, lean cuts of beef, poultry, fish, nuts, seeds, whole grains, beans, eggs, and yogurt.

If you're dieting, rapid weight loss can lead to nutritional deficiencies resulting in not-so-healthy, lackluster fingernails. Try to lose no more than 2 pounds per week and adhere to a balanced diet.

Stress zaps your body of iron and vitamins A, B, and C — necessary nutrients for strong, straight nails. It also reduces blood flow to your fingertips, leaving your nails looking pale.

Include in your diet foods such as pumpkin seeds and flaxseeds, and evening primrose or borage oils. These are rich in essential fatty acids that strengthen nails and moisturize surrounding skin.

Zinc, sulfur, and silica are important minerals known to fortify nails. Include broccoli, onions, garlic, spirulina, barley grass, alfalfa, dandelion, nuts, whole grains, and apples in your daily diet.

Biotin and folic acid, especially important B vitamins, help prevent and heal peeling, brittle nails.

A daily glass of calcium-rich carrot juice is a delicious way to strengthen bones, teeth, and nails. Calcium-fortified soy milk and skim cow's milk are also good sources.

43

Reflexology for Stress Relief

Reflexology is a science based on the idea that there are reflexes in the feet and hands relative to all the organs, functions, and parts of the human body. Applying pressure with your thumbs and forefingers to these points can bring about amazing results. Reflexology promotes stress relief, normalizes bodily functions, improves circulation, and relieves pain.

Let's Unwind

Your feet are actually more sensitive and receptive to touch than your hands because they contain a wealth of nerve endings, approximately 7,200 in each foot. Also, because they, unlike your hands, are not constantly exposed to the elements, they are highly responsive to the calming, tranquilizing effects induced by a reflexology session.

I can't possibly show you how to perform all of the various reflexology steps here. But the following are two basic reflexology techniques that can easily be performed at home to bring relief after a stressful day. Reflexology should always be practiced on a dry foot.

Big-Toe Stimulation: This exercise increases blood flow to your brain, pituitary and pineal glands, and neck. It also relieves neck stress and relaxes the mind. Holding the ball of your foot between your thumb (on the sole) and index fingers (on the top), "walk" down and "walk" up each of the five zones in your big toe. To find the zones, draw four evenly spaced vertical lines from the tip to the base of the big toe. In order to "thumb walk," you must make an inchwormlike motion with the outside edge of your thumb by bending the thumb repeatedly as you climb up or down, simultaneously applying pressure.

Solar Plexus Press: "The solar plexus is referred to as the 'nerve switchboard' of the body, as it is the main storage area for stress. Applying pressure to this reflex will always bring about a feeling of relaxation," say Inge Dougans and Suzanne Ellis, authors of *The Art of Reflexology*. To find the solar plexus reflex, grasp the top of your foot and gently squeeze the metatarsals (the five bones along the midportion of your foot that connect to each toe). A depression will have formed just under the ball of your foot and in the center. This depression represents the solar plexus reflex. Press your thumb into this spot and hold for a few seconds. Release. You can also work your thumb in small circular motions, first clockwise, then counterclockwise. Finish by pressing and holding again.

HEAL YOUR SKIN THROUGH STRESS REDUCTION

Skin disorders such as eczema, psoriasis, acne, hives, excess perspiration, and a pale complexion can be triggered or worsened by stress. Techniques for reducing stress include exercise, ample sleep, facial and body massage, reflexology, deep breathing, biofeedback, reiki, time with close friends and family, and recreation.

Make Your Bedroom a Haven

It's a fact: The average human spends more time in the bedroom than any other room in the house, and frequently this room is designated for sleeping and nothing else. It doesn't have to be that way. Your bedroom should be your personal haven, with an ambience that is conducive to relaxation, meditation, reading, and romance.

Create a Private Retreat

Forget white walls — how boring! Experiment with color. If you're timid, try a pastel shade first; if you're more dramatic, try a bolder color. Use your imagination!

Plants can add serenity and interest to a bedroom, not to mention oxygenating the air and adding a natural look. If your furnishings are sparse, plant a large palm, benjamin ficus, or rubber tree in a decorative pot and place it in front of a big sunny window. Take care to keep it out of reach of children and pets.

If your bedroom is spacious enough to accommodate a chair and ottoman or a chaise lounge, then by all means invest in one. These chairs offer the utmost in comfort and actually provide a come-hither invitation to recline and read or nap.

Invest in high-quality flannel, pima cotton, or satin sheets. Sleeping should be as cozy or sensual as possible.

Keep a daily journal on your nightstand. Each night, pause and write down your reflections of the day. It's a good way to unwind and allow the day's business to drain away.

Keep a tea tray next to your bed or chair and stock it with your favorite herbal or regular teas. Fill a beautiful ceramic or pottery teapot with boiling water, bring it into your bedroom, and brew a pot of relaxation.

Place several scented candles of varying heights in front of a mirror, perhaps on your dresser. Light them before a romantic encounter to scent the air, and watch the light flicker and dance.

Rediscover the joys of an imaginative journey through reading. Keep a selection of soul-nourishing books at your bedside.

Make or purchase several velvet or chenille throw pillows that coordinate with your bedroom colors. They're cushy and soft and make a great back support for reading in bed.

Designate a special area in your bedroom for practicing yoga, meditation, or simple stretching exercises. These are wonderful ways to ease into or end your day.

Finally, don't forget music. It can calm you down, rev you up, make you feel like dancing or singing, wake you up, or lull you to sleep.

45

Surround Yourself with Fragrance

Because fragrance so strongly touches the brain's emotional centers, it can dramatically affect mood and memory. Fresh-baked chocolate chip cookies, an evergreen forest in summer, an ocean breeze, a newborn puppy — all evoke wonderful memories that can be rekindled in an instant at the first whiff of the scent.

Stop and Smell the Roses

My favorite fragrant flowers are the double rosa rugosa, lilac, lavender, honeysuckle, wild azalea, hyacinth, privet, gardenia, lily-of-the-valley, freesia, rose, verbena, and orange blossom. This mixture of shrubs, bushes, perennials, and vines produces flowers with intense, heady, intoxicatingly sweet aromas.

To scent your percale sheets and make them feel more like silk, sprinkle with a light dusting of your favorite perfumed dusting powder.

Need an instant, cooling energy boost? Spray the soles of your feet with chilled cologne or chilled peppermint or rose geranium herbal water.

Place a cake of your favorite perfumed soap into your lingerie drawer — or your desk at work, for that matter. Every time you open the drawer, you'll receive a waft of fragrance.

Citrusy Room Freshener

Essential oils of grapefruit and lemon combine to make a light, sweet, refreshing spray that will simultaneously neutralize any unpleasant smells (especially pet odors) while lifting your spirits. Economical and chemical-free!

    ½ cup distilled water
    1 teaspoon essential oil of lemon
    1 teaspoon essential oil of grapefruit

Pour the blend into a 4-ounce glass mister. Shake well before using to mist the air throughout your home.

46

Mask Yourself

Facial masks can be made from myriad natural ingredients and are used to deep-clean, tone, exfoliate, or soften the skin, or to stimulate a sluggish complexion. Masks should always be applied to freshly cleansed, damp skin. Try to lie or sit down and rest while using the mask; relaxation will only further the benefits of the treatment.

Uncover the Real You

To reestablish that "peaches and cream" glow in normal, dry, or highly sensitive skin, mash half of a very ripe, small peach with 2 teaspoons of heavy cream. Apply the paste to your face and neck and leave on for 30 minutes. Rinse with warm water.

Need an instant mask that's calming and soothing for sunburned or irritated skin that's either normal or oily? Grab the bottle of milk of magnesia from the medicine chest and apply it in a thin layer over your entire face, throat, and chest. Let it dry for 5 to 10 minutes. Rinse with warm water. Follow with a light moisturizer.

An apple a day keeps dry-skin buildup away! Apples contain malic acid, a mild alpha-hydroxy acid that sloughs off the surface layer of dead skin cells. In the blender, mix half of a small peeled apple with a tiny amount of water until smooth. Apply the pulpy liquid with a cotton ball to your face, throat, and chest. Allow to dry for 15 to 20 minutes. Rinse with warm water. This mask can be used by all skin types.

Brewer's Yeast Circulation Booster

This mask can be used by all skin types. It brings a very rosy glow to the skin and helps chase away that winter "pasty" look.

- 1 tablespoon brewer's yeast
- 2 teaspoons water (oily skin), 1 or 2 percent milk (normal skin), or cream (dry skin)

Combine the ingredients to form a smooth paste. You may need more or less liquid than called for, depending on the brand of yeast. Spread this onto your face and throat in a thin layer; let dry. Rinse. This mask may tingle as it dries, which is normal. If it starts to sting, rinse it off immediately and follow with a good moisturizer.

47

Tips for Luscious Lips

Your lips, unlike the rest of your skin, contain no sebaceous (oil) glands or sweat glands and therefore cannot moisturize themselves. If lip tissue is damaged by heat, cold, drying lipsticks, smoking, too many happy-hour beverages, herpes, or other agents, the small amount of saliva that reaches your lips via the tip of the tongue will not be sufficient to prevent your lips from becoming dehydrated.

Pucker Up!

When venturing out into the sun, be it the beach or bright ski slope, don't forget to apply a lip balm with an SPF of 15 or higher.

Thick castor oil, an ingredient in lipstick, can be applied straight out of the bottle for a glossy look.

Slick on a bit of cocoa butter for a moisturizing, chocolate-flavored lip treat. Great for men and boys because it's colorless and not too shiny.

After brushing your teeth, gently brush your lips as well. "Not only does it take away any chapping, but it plumps up the lip temporarily for that sought-after 'pouty' look," says Diane Irons, author of *The World's Best-Kept Beauty Secrets*.

Apply a lip balm frequently throughout the day to create a moisture-resistant barrier on your lips that will help prevent moisture loss.

Keep hydrated! Make sure to drink lots of water throughout the day.

A dab of honey on your lips will act as a humectant, drawing moisture from the air to your skin, keeping your lips soft, plump, and kissably sweet.

A dab of vegetable glycerin mixed with vitamin E or wheat germ oil makes an effective, nourishing moisture barrier.

48

Learn to Love Lavender

From ancient Greece to modern times, lavender has been one of the most common and widely used cultivated herbs. And it's no wonder, because it's one of the most versatile, too. All forms of lavender — essential oil, dried or fresh flowers, aromatic hydrosol, and tea — are safe to use on all skin types, even young children's delicate skin.

The Benefits of Lavender

Grow a patch of lavender. Plant a few mounds in a sunny spot around a garden bench or large stone or log. On a hot summer's day, have a seat in your lavender patch. Brush your hands against the plant and inhale the delightful scent wafting through the breeze. Lavender is recommended for people who experience constant stress and overstimulation and find it difficult to relax and unwind.

The essential oil of these lovely, purple, highly fragrant flowers can soothe your soul without sapping your energy. To enhance concentration and promote mental clarity, place a drop on your wrist, the palms of your hands, or the nape of your neck and breathe deeply.

Lavender is a potent antiseptic. Add 2 drops of essential oil of lavender to 1 teaspoon of soybean, almond, olive, or hazelnut oil or aloe vera juice and apply the mixture directly to burns, sunburns, abrasions, insect stings, or inflamed pimples to cleanse and disinfect.

Make a skin-softening bath sachet. Combine ¼ cup dried lavender flowers, ¼ cup instant, powdered whole milk, and ¼ cup oatmeal. Place into a 3-by-5-inch muslin drawstring bag. Toss the bag into the bathwater so that the ingredients can release their skin-pampering properties. Rub the sachet over your entire body to cleanse and hydrate dry skin.

Improve your mood. Purchase a bottle of lavender aromatic hydrosol — a watery by-product of essential oil distillation — and spray a fine mist onto your face and hair, and into the surrounding air. Inhale the vapors. The chemical components of the lavender plant have the ability to alter the emotions by influencing the sense of smell, which triggers the region of the brain that deals with memory and mood.

Old-Fashioned Lavender Vinegar

Sprinkle a dash of this fragrant vinegar onto a salad for a delectable departure from your ordinary dressing, or use 1 part vinegar to 8 parts water as a facial toner or hair rinse. This recipe makes approximately 2 cups of vinegar.

- 1 cup fresh or ½ cup dried lavender flowers and leaves
- 2 teaspoons lemon zest
- 2 cups raw apple cider vinegar

Place the lavender and lemon zest in a clean quart-size canning jar and pour in the unheated vinegar. Cover the top with plastic wrap, then screw on the lid and store in a dark, cool place for two to four weeks. Shake daily. Strain the vinegar, bottle in a decorative container, and use as you would ordinary vinegar.

Happy is he who hath the power to gather wisdom from a flower.

— Anonymous

49

Make an Herbal Dream Pillow

Adream pillow is a fragrant, soft little pillow filled with the herbs traditionally used to calm nightmares; evoke colorful, exotic, or peaceful dreams; or simply help you sleep more soundly. Tuck a pillow into your pillowcase while you sleep and let the fairies and dream weavers lead you into the land of Nod.

Choose your favorite mixture and follow the instructions below for making a dream pillow. All herbs used are in dried form, unless stated otherwise.

Scented Slumber

For Soothing, Outdoor Dreams: ¼ cup fresh or dried spruce or balsam fir needles, ¼ cup fresh or

dried pine needles cut into ½-inch pieces, ¼ cup
mugwort, ¼ cup lemon balm.

For Romantic Dreams: ¼ cup lavender, ¼ cup
rose petals, ¼ cup whole chamomile, 2 tablespoons hops, and 2 tablespoons catnip. If you
have cats, you might want to omit the catnip; my
cat, Toby, discovered this particular flannel-
encased pillow and took it away for his own bed!

For Vivid, Colorful Dreams: ½ cup lemongrass,
¼ cup marigold flowers, ¼ cup mugwort.

Dream Pillow

*This pillow is easy to make and perfect for gift giving.
Sweet dreams!*

Choose one of the above blends or create your own
favorite mixture

1. To make a quick pillow, buy a 3-by-5-inch or 4-by-6-
inch plain, muslin cloth drawstring bag and fill it with your
herbs. Tie closed. You can also use the plain bag as the liner
and cover it in a softer, more decorative fabric such as flannel, silk, satin, or velveteen.

2. To make your own custom pillow cover, cut an 11-inch
square piece of fabric and hem the raw edges to ½ inch with
stitching.

3. Place the herb-filled liner bag onto the wrong side of the
decorative fabric and wrap the bag like a piece of hard candy.
Tie both ends of the fabric with a piece of ribbon. Refill the
herb liner every two or three months.

50

Words of Wisdom

There are a multitude of self-help books out there to treat the mind, body, and spirit. But sometimes the most important concepts to remember are the simplest: lessons you learned from your parents, teachers, children, or even your own experiences. Take the time to appreciate what you have and recall a few wise words that will inspire you throughout the day.

Live Well

Trust in yourself. Your creativity will flow and life will be easier to handle.

Raise your energy level and ability to concentrate by practicing deep breathing. Breathe in deeply and exhale completely.

Exercise on a regular basis.

Bathe weekly in your favorite essential oils.

Eat more fresh fruits and vegetables.

Choose challenge and change.

Ask for hugs from those you love.

Do something that will make you feel good about yourself; have a massage, buy yourself a special treat, or take a day off.

Talk to and love the child inside you.

Stop blaming yourself and others.

Begin each day on a positive note. Buy a book of

daily devotions or inspirational mottos and read one every morning when you arise.

Ask someone you trust to tell you what they like about you.

Communicate with nature. Take walks, explore the nearby woods, or even just sit outside on the grass and appreciate the sights, sounds, and smells.

Sit quietly and listen to your heart; it often gives the best advice.

SELF-AFFIRMATIONS

Practice self-affirmations every day to keep your perspective positive and uplifting. Here are some examples:

* ✳ "I now trust myself completely."

* ✳ "I am a smart and talented go-getter."

* ✳ "I am calm and relaxed no matter what the circumstances."

* ✳ "I am at peace."

* ✳ "I will not worry, no matter what comes my way today."

* ✳ "I can do anything I set my mind to."

Index

The Love of Christ

The Love of Christ

SPIRITUAL COUNSELS

Mother Teresa

of Calcutta

Edited by Georges Gorrée and Jean Barbier

1817

Harper & Row, Publishers, San Francisco

Cambridge, Hagerstown, New York, Philadelphia,
London, Mexico City, São Paulo, Sydney

Parts I and II were translated by John A. Otto from the original French edition, *Tu M'Apportes l'Amour* (Paris: Les Editions du Centurion, 1975). Parts III and IV are are based on Mother Teresa's original English documents.

FIRST EDITION

Designer: Jim Mennick

Library of Congress Cataloging in Publication Data

Teresa, Mother, 1910–

  THE LOVE OF CHRIST.

  "Parts 1 and 2 translated by John A. Otto from the original French edition, Tu m'apportes l'amour (Paris: Les Editions du Centurion, 1975). Parts 2–3 are based on Mother Teresa's original English documents"—Verso t.p.

  1. Christian life—Catholic authors.   I. Gorrée, Georges, 1908– .   II. Barbier, Jean.   III. Title.

| BX2350.2.T467 | 1982 | 248.4'82 | 81–23746 |
| ISBN 0–06–068229–9 | | | AACR2 |

---

82   83   84   85   86   10   9   8   7   6   5   4   3   2

Contents

Introduction

Mother Teresa speaks little, publishes even less. Of necessity, however, she carries on a large volume of correspondence. In addition, she is asked for many interviews and sometimes has to speak in public (whenever her work is recognized by a prize of one kind or another). In this varied activity, in which she is generally spontaneous and uninhibited by the fear of repetition, what she projects is the faith by which she lives and love that impels her.

Appearing in this work are words of Mother Teresa. Some of them have been gathered by attentive listeners. Others are drawn from her letters, or from directives to her Co-Workers, or from her commentary on the constitutions of the Missionary Sisters and Brothers of Charity. Our aim has been to reproduce her simple and straightforward language, which concentrates on the truly essential and reveals the beauty of a totally dedicated life as well as the almost unbearable realities of misery and suffering.

As an aid to the reader, some division into parts had to be made. The division, in the nature of the case, is more or less arbitrary. Mother Teresa's life, however, is not divided or compartmentalized. It is an indivisible whole, its source and strength the twofold commandment of love of God and love of neighbor.

Acknowledgments

Some of the material in Parts I and II is drawn from Malcolm Muggeridge's *Something Beautiful for God* (New York, Harper & Row, 1971) and the authors' earlier work on Mother Teresa, *Amour sans frontière*.

The text of Parts III and IV is from unpublished material that was supplied by the Missionaries of Charity.

In addition, we have drawn upon interviews given by Mother Teresa and articles by various journalists such as Ralph Rolls and Sandro Bordignon.

PART I

God

MY LIFE, BUT NEVER MY FAITH

"Lord, give me this vision of faith, and my work will never become monotonous."

So prays Mother Teresa, in prayer both strong and confident. Ralph Rolls asked her what she would do if a country where she worked demanded that she give up her faith. She replied:*

No one can take my faith from me. If, in order to spread the love of Christ among the poor and neglected, there were no alternative but to remain in that country, I would remain—but I would not renounce my faith. I am prepared to *give up my life but never my faith.*

Voluntarily choosing this hazardous and humanly wretched life is the measure of her faith. What else explains it? Certainly not the results,

---

* Material in italics is commentary by the authors. The rest of the text is Mother Teresa's own words.

> *which, as the world counts, would have to be judged small.*

We realize that what we are accomplishing is a drop in the ocean. But if this drop were not in the ocean, it would be missed. If we did not have our schools in the quarters of the poor—they are small, primary schools, where we teach the children to like school and how to keep themselves clean—if we did not have these small schools, the thousands of children who benefit from them would be left in the streets.

It is the same with our Home for the Dying. If we did not have this home, those whom we bring in would die in the streets. I believe it is worth the trouble to have this home, if only for the comparatively few we can handle, so that they may die with some dignity and in the peace of God.

> *Another secret of Mother Teresa's life is her power of perseverance. According to the French priest-orator Lacordaire, to persevere one must be as "loving as a mother and as hard as a diamond." Mother Teresa finds the explanation in her faith:*

Faith is a gift of God. Without it there would be no life. Our work, to bear fruit, to belong only to God, to be deserving, must be built on faith.

Christ said: "I was hungry, I was naked, I was sick, I was homeless, and you did that for me."* All our work is based on faith in these words.

---

* Matthew 25:35–40: " ' For I was hungry and you gave me food, I was thirsty and you gave me drink, I was a stranger and you welcomed me, I was naked and you clothed me, I was sick and you visited me, I was in prison and you came to me.' Then the righteous will answer him, 'Lord, when did we see thee hungry and feed thee,

If faith is lacking, it is because there is too much selfishness, too much concern for personal gain. For faith to be true, it has to be generous and loving. Love and faith go together; they complete each other.

| *But she does not impose her faith.*

It is our prayer that Christ communicate His light and life to each of us and through us to the world of misery. We hope that the poor, whatever their beliefs, seeing us will be drawn to Christ and will want us to come to them, into their lives.

> *Mother Teresa's faith is something so absolute and so solid that she would rather see herself and her work destroyed than forget her faith or doubt it for a moment. The intensity of her faith is a phenomenon that is attracting the attention of the world and making history. Faith exudes from her whole being, faith that is truth.*
>
> *Though reason retains its importance in the exercise of faith and following Christ does not mean its abandonment, the young, beset with problems, sometimes forgo the reasoning process. In the case of Mother Teresa, at least, they seem to follow her implicitly.*
>
> *When she decided to join a march of seven kilometers through the streets of Milan for the purpose of arousing support for solidarity with the*

---

or thirsty and give thee drink? And when did we see thee a stranger and welcome thee, or naked and clothe thee? And when did we see thee sick or in prison and visit thee?' And the King will answer them, 'Truly, I say to you as you did it to one of the least of these my brethren, you did it to me.' "

> *Third World, for her, according to the French journalist Bordignon, it was a symbolic gesture. The organizers had been preoccupied with the details of the march, but the news that she would participate transformed it into a procession of faith. Everyone was struck by the expression on her face, the ascetical features which, like her words, spoke the force of truth. Afterwards she was received by Cardinal Giovanni Colombo, archbishop of Milan, to whom she said:*

Before God we are all poor.

> *Why this march? Why would thousands of young people assemble at the cathedral square to begin with Mother Teresa this seven-kilometer march without fanfare, without banners? Why would the young march for something they did not clearly understand, or if they did, still hesitated to admit it for fear of being challenged?*

The young are the builders of tomorrow. Youth today is in search of selflessness, and when it finds it, is prepared to embrace it.

In Harlem a young woman of a wealthy family came to us in a taxicab and told me: "I have given everything to the poor and have come to follow Christ."

Sometimes Jesus receives unusual attention. One evening in London I had a telephone call from the police: "Mother Teresa, there is a women in the streets very drunk, who is calling for you." We went to find her and on the way back she said to me: "Mother Teresa, Christ changed water into wine so that we would have some to drink." And she was very, very drunk!

> *Ralph Rolls put this question to Mother Teresa: "Is it important for you to be a Catholic?"*

Yes. For me and for every individual, according to the grace God has given to each.

> *It matters little, then, to what part of the Christian church we belong?*

No, it is important for the individual. If the individual thinks and believes that his or her way is the only way to God, if they do not know any other way, do not doubt and so do not feel the need to look elsewhere, then that is their way of salvation, the way that God comes into their life. But from the moment that a soul receives the grace to know God it must begin to seek. And if it does not seek, it moves away from the right road. But God gives to all souls that He creates a chance to meet Him and to accept Him or reject Him.

> *Is unity among Christians important?*

Yes, because Christians represent a light for others. If we are Christians, we must resemble Christ. I believe this very deeply. Gandhi once said if Christians had lived their Christian life completely, there would be no Hindus left in India. People expect us to live our Christian life fully.

> *The followers of other religions, Moslems, Hindus, are they also blessed by God and does God work through them too?*

God has His own means and ways of working in the hearts of people, and we do not know how close they are to Him. But in their actions we always have a clue to their attitude toward Him, whether or not they are responsive to Him. Moslem, Hindu, or Christian, the way you live your life is the measure of your belonging to God. We cannot condemn or judge, or speak words that might hurt. Perhaps a person has never heard of Christianity; if so, we do not know in what manner God appears in this soul and in what way He has this soul serve His purpose. By what right, then, can we condemn anyone?

I LOOK UPON HIM, HE LOOKS UPON ME

It is not possible to engage in the apostolate without being a soul of prayer, without consciously forgetting oneself and submitting to God's will. We must be conscious of our oneness with Christ, as He was of His oneness with His Father. Our activity is truly apostolic only to the extent that we let Christ work in us and through us, with all His power, all His desire, and all His love.

> *A soul of prayer can make progress without recourse to words, by learning to listen, to be present to Christ, and to look toward Him.*

Often we do not receive what we prayed and hoped for because we did not fix our attention and our hearts on Christ, through whom our prayers come to God. Many times a deep and fervent gaze upon Christ is the best prayer. *I look upon Him, He looks upon me* is the most perfect prayer.

| *Her prayer speaks mercy, kindness, patience.*

"Lord, grant that I may always bear in mind the very great dignity of my vocation, and all its responsibilities. Never let me dishonor it by being cold, or unkind, or impatient."

Love prayer. Feel often the need to pray, and take the trouble to pray. It is by praying often that you will pray better. Prayer enlarges the heart until it is capable of containing the gift that God makes of Himself. Ask and seek: your heart will grow capable of receiving Him and holding on to Him.

| *The need to discover Christ in the sick forms part*
| *of her daily prayer.*

"Jesus, my suffering Lord, grant that today and every day I may see You in the person of Your sick ones, and that in caring for them I may serve You. Grant also that even in the guise of the fretful, the demanding, the unreasonable, I may still recognize You and say: My suffering Jesus, how sweet it is to serve You.

"Lord, give me this vision of faith, and my work will never become monotonous. I will find joy in indulging the moods and gratifying the desires of all the poor who suffer.

"O dear sick one, how much dearer still you are to me because you represent Christ. What a privilege I have to be able to tend to you.

"O God, since You are Jesus in his suffering, deign

also to be to me a patient Jesus, overlooking my faults, seeing only my intentions, which are to love You and to serve You in the person of each of Your children who suffers. Lord, increase my faith.

"Bless my efforts and my work, now and always."

| *"How do you pray?" Bordignon asked her.*

We begin our day by seeing Christ in the consecrated bread, and throughout the day we continue to see Him in the torn bodies of our poor. We pray, that is, through our work, performing it with Jesus, for Jesus, and upon Jesus.

The poor are our prayer. They carry God in them. Prayer means praying everything, praying the work.

| *What consolation do you find in your work?*

We meet the Lord who hungers and thirsts, in the poor . . . and the poor could be you or I or any person kind enough to show us his or her love and to come to our place.

IN SILENCE, HE HEARS US, HE SPEAKS TO US

It is very hard to pray if one does not know how. We must help ourselves to learn.

The most important thing is silence. Souls of prayer are souls of deep silence. We cannot place ourselves directly in God's presence without imposing upon ourselves interior and exterior silence. That is why we must accustom ourselves to stillness of the soul, of the eyes, of the tongue.

God is the friend of silence. We need to find God, but

we cannot find Him in noise, in excitement. See how nature, the trees, the flowers, the grass grow in deep silence. See how the stars, the moon, and the sun move in silence.

Is not our mission to bring God to the poor in the streets? Not a dead God but a living God, a God of love. The apostles said: "We will devote ourselves to prayer and to the ministry of the word."

The more we receive in our silent prayer, the more we can give in our active life. Silence gives us a new way of looking at everything. We need this silence in order to touch souls. The essential thing is not what we say but what God says to us and what He says through us.

Jesus is always waiting for us in silence. *In this silence He listens to us; it is there that He speaks to our souls.* And there, we hear His voice. Interior silence is very difficult, but we must make the effort to pray. In this silence we find a new energy and a real unity. God's energy becomes ours, allowing us to perform things well. There is unity of our thoughts with His thoughts, unity of our prayers with His prayers, unity of our actions with His actions, of our life with His life.

Our words are useless unless they come from the bottom of the heart. Words that do not give the light of Christ only make the darkness worse.

Make every effort to walk in the presence of God, to see God in everyone you meet, and to live your morning meditation throughout the day. In the streets in particular, radiate the joy of belonging to God, of living with Him and being His. For this reason, in the streets, in the shelters, in your work, you should al-

ways be praying with all your heart and all your soul.
Maintain the silence that Jesus maintained for thirty
years at Nazareth, and that He still maintains in the
tabernacle, interceding for us. Pray like the Virgin
Mary, who kept all things in her heart through prayer
and meditation, and still does, as mediatrix of all
graces.

Christ's teaching is so simple that even a little
child can learn it. The apostles said: "Teach us to
pray." Jesus answered: "When you pray, say, Our
Father . . ."

ALONE, WE CAN DO NOTHING

> *Mother Teresa chooses to serve. But service she
> understands as an instrument that is more effec-
> tive the more humble it is.*

That is why we should be able to summon our courage and say in all sincerity: "I can do all things in
Him, because it is He who strengthens me."

This assertion of St. Paul should give you great
confidence in the realization of your work, or rather
God's work, in its efficacy and perfection in Jesus and
for Jesus. Be also convinced that alone, of yourself,
you can do nothing, and have nothing except sin,
weakness and misery; that all the natural gifts and
gifts of grace we have were given to us by God.

We can see the humility of Jesus in the crib, in the
Exile in Egypt and His hidden life, in the inability to
make Himself understood by people, in the abandonment by the apostles, in the hatred of His enemies

among the Jews, in all the bitter sufferings of the
Passion, and now in His acts of constant humility in
the tabernacle, where he reduces Himself to such a
small piece of bread that the priest can hold Him
between two fingers.

*To Malcolm Muggeridge she made the request
that his study about her work not be in the nature
of a biography of herself:*

The life of Christ was not written during his lifetime, yet He did the greatest work on earth—He redeemed the world and taught mankind to love His
Father. The work is His work and to remain so, all of
us are but his instruments, who do our little bit and
pass by.*

Let there be no pride or vanity in the work. The
work is God's work, the poor are God's poor. Let us put
ourselves completely under the power and influence
of Jesus, so that He may think with our minds, work
with our hands, for we can do all things if His strength
is with us.

Our mission is to convey the love of God, who is not
a dead God but a living God.

*Not a God of facile or premature solutions that
seem reasonable but sometimes wound the sensitivity of people in distress. Not a dead God, served
merely from a sense of duty, a burden on our conscience that we attempt to load onto the shoulders
of others. But a living God, a God of mercy, of*

---

* Malcolm Muggeridge, *Something Beautiful for God* (New York:
Harper & Row, 1971), p. 15.

compassion, who in Jesus Christ took the form of
man and became a member of the poor.

Mother Teresa teaches us that the desire to serve
the poor requires that we acknowledge the misery
in ourselves, our own insufficiency and radical
poverty.

We must accept our vulnerability and limitations in regard to others. This is essential in gain-
ing their confidence. We cannot expect to help others from the "outside."

Learn to be quiet so that the other can speak.
Forget about rules that relegate the oppressed to
the margins of society, leaving them in their isolation. Hope with the captives of unjust social conditions, who have nothing but their untold wants.
Hope with "prisoners," those overwhelmed by
physical, moral, or spiritual misery.

Mother Teresa permits herself to be "touched"
by the untouchables, those whom we too quickly
consign to the ranks of the irrecoverable, the hope-
less. She permits herself to be "disarmed" by the
exigent cry of people. Often it is the "marginaliza-
tion," the rejection, the lack of understanding
that causes people to withdraw into themselves.

It is not easy to be poor with the poor, to surrender power and the confidence in our "solutions,"
our "normality."

It is not easy to visit a person in his or her
isolation, to break down the barriers that separate
the world of the "haves" from the world of the
"have-nots."

It takes a great deal of humility to acknowledge

*one's limitations, one's helplessness or inade-
quacy.*

One of Mother Teresa's favorite thoughts is:

With Jesus, everything is possible because God is
love.

*Despite the publicity and attention that surround
her—which she does not want and tries to discour-
age*—Mother Teresa moves about in her unas-
suming manner, slight and almost unnoticed
amid the others.*

*When one finds her, in an old building on the
grounds of the Kali Temple, it is difficult to pick
her out from the other Sisters. Nothing suggests
that she is the founder of a congregation of religious with foundations all over the world.*

*She finds it painful to get ready for an inter-
view. She confesses:*

For me, it is more difficult than bathing a leper, if
it comes to that.

*Before a television interview she can be seen seated
in a dim corner behind the curtain, fingering her
large beads as she waits to speak to thousands, or
millions.*

---

*Mother Teresa was recently quoted to the effect that the publicity
that has fallen on her since receiving the Nobel Prize was interfer-
ing with her work of service to the poor and therefore she would not
"participate in any more receptions" (United News of India, 2 April
1980). Nevertheless, her work continues to be recognized. In April
1980 she received the Bharat Ratna (Jewel of India), India's highest
civilian award, for her "exceptional service of charity" to the poor
of India's cities.—Translator's note.

> *She does not put her thoughts on paper or make notes. She does not have the gift for that kind of preparation; she relies for guidance on her rosary.*

GIVE ME TO DRINK

> *Jesus thirsts for love. This same God who says that He does not need to tell us if He is hungry did not hesitate to ask for a drink of water from the Samaritan woman. But in saying, "Give me to drink," it was the love of His creature that the Creator asked for.*
>
> *"What you do to the least of my brethren, you do to me." Mother Teresa develops this thought:*

When I was hungry, you gave me to eat.
When I was thirsty, you gave me to drink.

Whatsoever you do to the least of my brethren, that you do unto me.
Now enter the house of my Father.

When I was homeless, you opened your doors.
When I was naked, you gave me your coat.

When I was weary, you helped me find rest.
When I was anxious, you calmed all my fears.

When I was little, you taught me to read.
When I was lonely, you gave me your love.

When in a prison, you came to my cell.
When on a sick bed, you cared for my needs.

In a strange country, you made me at home.
Seeking employment, you found me a job.

Hurt in a battle, you bound up my wounds.
Searching for kindness, you held out your hand.

When I was Negro, or Chinese, or white, and
Mocked and insulted, you carried my cross.

When I was aged, you bothered to smile.
When I was restless, you listened and cared.

You saw me covered with spittle and blood,
You knew my features, though grimy with sweat.

When I was laughed at, you stood by my side.
When I was happy, you shared in my joy.*

We must live this life, this hard life, to be able to continue to work among the people. The work is our only way of expressing our love for God. Our love must pour on someone. The people are the means of expressing our love of God.

God gives what is needed. He gives to the flowers and the birds, and to everything that He has created in the universe. And the little children are His life. There can never be enough of them.

If the work is seen only through our own eyes and our own means, obviously we are not up to the task. But in Christ we can do all things. That is why this work has become possible, because we are convinced that He, Christ, works with us and through us, in the poor and for the poor.

The work is only an expression of the love we have for God. Loving others is an expression of our love for God.**

---

* Reprinted from Muggeridge, *Something Beautiful for God,* pp. 78–79.
** Letter from Mother Teresa to Co-Workers, December, 1971.

We must all be witnesses of Christ. Christ is the
vine and we are the branches. Without us, there
would be no fruit. This is something to bear in mind.
God is the vinedresser to all of us. Christ made no
distinction between priests and brothers, sisters and
laywomen, no distinction as witness-bound. We must
all be witnesses of Christ's compassion, Christ's love,
to our families, to our neighbors, to the towns or cities
where we reside, and to the world in which we live.

Only in heaven will we know how much we owe to
the poor, because on account of them we were able to
love God more.*

> *For the poor, Mother Teresa renounces and emp-
> ties herself. Were it not for Jesus Christ, this re-
> nunciation would seem absurd, an abdication of
> reason. But the poor invest it with Jesus Christ.
> Love of Jesus is the light that shines in her life
> and lends her a kind of spiritual luminosity
> which radiates from her in spite of herself and
> trails her wherever she goes. It lights up her wrin-
> kled face and is the reason why the world is in-
> trigued, yes, fascinated.*
>
> *Jesus is the one she wants her Co-Workers to
> bring to the world but especially to the poor.*

A Co-Worker must be capable of bringing Jesus to
people. For that, we must remain close to God. We
should have a daily holy hour of prayer and meditation. Even where we are not many, we could have it

---

* Mother Teresa, at the first national congress of Co-Workers held
in Salt Lake City, Utah.

in our parish church, or wherever we are. If we truly love the poor, our first contact must be with Jesus, in the blessed sacrament. Then it will be easy to bring our love for Jesus to the poor.

> *"I am the bread of life; he who comes to me shall not hunger, and he who believes in me shall never thirst" (John 6:35).*
>
> *Mother Teresa strives to be one "body" with Jesus; her "food" is to praise His Name. To be one "body" with Jesus means to let oneself be touched and healed by His mercy, to have eyes to see,*
> *ears to hear,*
> *tongue to speak,*
> *to attack moral and physical corruption, to relieve spiritual and bodily paralysis.*
>
> *The "Body" of Christ is the prism through which she sees the body of the neighbor.*

Because we cannot see Christ, we cannot express our love to Him in person. But our neighbor we can see, and we can do for him or her what we would love to do for Jesus if He were visible.

Let us be open to God so that He can use us. Let us put love into our actions, beginning in the family, in the neighborhood, in the street. It is difficult, but there is where the work begins. We are co-workers of Christ, a fruitbearing branch of the vine.*

> *The street! With its surprises, its dens, hovels, and teeming misery! This where poverty roots. No*

---

* Mother Teresa, on receiving the Templeton Prize in London.

> *need for explanations, for big words. My brother or*
> *sister is there, waiting.*
>
> *The thoughts of the heart, does one write them*
> *down? That would be to rationalize them, to make*
> *them serve where they cannot serve. Love does not*
> *wait for explanations. It goes to work, a light, a*
> *force that finds new ways to meet the hopelessness*
> *of the old.*

We can work, but we cannot do it without God's
help. This we receive in our daily mass, when He gives
us strength through His bread.

> *She insists, to the chagrin of the world, that in*
> *dealing with the poor the tables are turned: it is*
> *not the poor who are indebted to us but we who are*
> *indebted to them.*
>
> *Mother Teresa explains what she considers to be*
> *the essential difference between the Christian and*
> *non-Christian conceptions of love.*

Non-Christians and Christians both do social work,
but non-Christians do it for something while we do it
for someone. This accounts for the respect, the love
and devotion, because we do it for God. That is why we
try to do it as beautifully as possible. We are in continual contact with Christ in His work, just as we are in
contact with Him at mass and in the blessed sacrament. There, Jesus has the appearance of bread. But
in the world of misery, in the torn bodies, in the children, it is the same Christ that we see, that we touch.

> *Accordingly, for Mother Teresa the two command-*
> *ments, love of God and love of neighbor, are*

> *fulfilled together; they are in fact inseparable. Her*
> *life is a monument to these two loves which are*
> *one. How, if we do not love God, can we love our*
> *neighbor; and how, if we do not love our neighbor,*
> *can we love God?*
>
> *She preaches Christ every moment of the day, by*
> *living in Him, through Him, and for Him.*
>
> *In 1956 Mother Teresa introduced the daily*
> *Holy Hour for her Co-Workers.*

To make a retreat, let Jesus work in you. Let there be exposition, scripture, silence.

Jesus asked his disciples to be with Him in His prayer. Finding them asleep, He said: "You can sleep now and take your rest. All is finished, the hour is come."

It is by an intuition of the heart that we are drawn to the Eucharist to come into His presence. The tabernacle is the guarantee that he has "pitched his tent" among us, perpetually.

The Eucharist is the sacrament of prayer, the source and summit of the Christian life. His presence before us hastens His cumulative presence in us. His presence imparts the Spirit to us, and lights up the shadows of our heart in deep communion.

The Holy Hour before the Eucharist should lead us to a "holy hour" with the poor, with those who will never be a human success and whose only consolation is Jesus. Our Eucharist is incomplete if it does not make us love and serve the poor. In receiving the communion of the poor, we discover our own poverty.

Every day we partake of the blessed sacrament, and

we have noticed a change come over our life. We have experienced a deeper love for Christ in the distressful appearance of the poor. We have come to a better understanding of ourselves and a better understanding of the poor—a clear sign of God's blessing.

Since we began this devotion, we have not diminished our work. We spend as much time at it as before, but now with greater understanding. People accept us more, now, because they hunger for God. Their need is not for us but for Jesus.

But how can one bring them Jesus unless oneself is intent on holiness?

I WILL

Holiness consists in doing God's will joyfully. Faithfulness makes saints. The spiritual life is a union with Jesus: the divine and the human giving themselves to each other. The only thing Jesus asks of us is to give ourselves to Him, in total poverty, and total self-forgetfulness.

The first step toward holiness is the will to become holy. Through a firm and upright will we love God, we choose God, we hasten to God, we reach Him, we have Him.

Often, under the pretext of humility, of trust, of abandonment, we can forget to use the strength of our will. Everything depends on these words: "I will" or "I will not." And into the expression "I will" I must put all my energy.

One cannot expect to become a saint without paying

the price, and the price is much renunciation, much temptation, much struggle and persecution, and all sorts of sacrifices. One cannot love God except at the cost of oneself.

If you learn the art of self-restraint and thoughtfulness, you will become more and more like Christ. His heart is all recompense, and He always thought of others. Jesus went about only doing good. At Cana, our Blessed Mother thought only of the needs of others and made them known to Jesus. The thoughtfulness of Jesus, Mary, and Joseph was so great that they made Nazareth a privileged abode of the Most High. If we had this same solicitude for one another, our communities would truly become a privileged abode of the Most High.

> *Mother Teresa is so closely united with God that God reveals Himself through her person. She is at once salt of the earth and light of the world. People who come to her are drawn to her in the same way that the crowds of Jerusalem were drawn to Christ.*
>
> *There is a brightness, a luminosity to Mother Teresa's love which overflows her Home for the Dying and transforms repellent and irritable creatures into human beings responding to love.*
>
> *A sort of "materialization" of this luminosity is reported by Malcolm Muggeridge, who was in charge of making a film about the Home for the Dying. The light inside was so dim that the cameraman said it was impossible to get a picture. It was decided to go ahead anyway. To the surprise*

> *of the technicians, the processed film showed the inside of the home and the dying bathed in beautiful soft light and was some of the best footage taken! What was the explanation for this "unnatural" occurrence?*
>
> *"I myself am absolutely convinced," says Malcolm Muggeridge, "that the technically unaccountable light is, in fact, the Kindly Light Newman refers to in his well-known hymn. . . . Mother Teresa's Home for the Dying is overflowing with love, as one senses immediately on entering it. This love is luminous, like the haloes artists have seen and made visible round the heads of the saints. I find it not at all surprising that the luminosity should register on a photographic film."**

Her light restores joy. Joy is a power, and the poor followed Jesus because power dwelled in Him, "went forth" from Him, flowed from His eyes, His hands, His body, totally given, present, to God, to people.

> *Malcolm Muggeridge relates that after his television interview with Mother Teresa the response of the British public was astounding. He himself received numerous letters, all of them as much as saying: "This woman spoke to me as no one ever has, and I feel I must help her."***

---

* Muggeridge, *Something Beautiful for God,* pp. 41–44.
** Ibid., p. 31.

PART II

The Other

LOVING THE OTHER

> *Mother Teresa's love is so great that she sees the neighbor as more beautiful than the reality suggests. She believes in love and produces love where there was none.*

The poor are God's gift; they are our love. Christ will not ask how much we did but how much love we put into what we did. There are many people who are spiritually poor. The spiritual poverty found in Europe, in America, is a heavy burden to bear. In these countries it is very difficult to convey a sense of God's love.

Our spiritual life is a life of dependence on God; its fruit is our work for the poor. We try to "pray" the work, doing it for Jesus, in Jesus and to Jesus.

The poor are "hope." By their courage they truly represent the hope of the world. They have taught us a different way of loving God by making us do our utmost to help them.

The role of the mother in the betterment of the individual is all-important. One of them complained to Mother Teresa that her children do not listen to her and asked what she should do. Mother Teresa replied:

Mothers are the heart of the home; they build family life by wanting, loving, and taking care of their children. One time in London I came upon a young boy who was on drugs. I said to him: "You are very young and should not be out in the street at this hour of the night." He replied: "My mother does not want me because I have long hair, and that is why I am here."

An hour later I returned to the same place and was told that the boy had taken four different drugs. He had been hurried to the hospital and very likely was already dead.

Recently, in L—, a young woman of twenty-one years, who had been scolded in the morning, attempted suicide later in the day by swallowing kerosene. Taken to the hospital, she said to the priest: "My mother chased me out of the house and I did not know where to go; so I thought the best thing would be to kill myself."

Much suffering of young people is attributable to the family, and particularly to mothers. Mothers make the home a center of love. Their role is sometimes hard, but there is the example of the Blessed Virgin, who teaches us to be good with our children. We Missionaries of Charity also have to be mothers and make our communities happy homes.

> *"Truly, I say to you, as you did it to one of the least*
> *of these my brethren, you did it to me" (Matthew*
> *25:40).*
>   *Mother Teresa's desire is to:*

Help people recognize God in the person of the poor.*

> *Though the possibility of knowing God rests on a*
> *certain resemblance between man and the God*
> *who took a human form, there is nothing in com-*
> *mon between the infinite nature of God and the*
> *finite nature of man.*

Let each Sister and Brother grow in resemblance to Christ, so that in the world of today He may still live His life of compassion and human kindness. Your love of Christ is so admirable! Keep the light of Christ always shining bright in your hearts. He is the Love to love.**

Love is a fruit always in season, and no limit is set. Everyone can reach this love.

Are we convinced of Christ's love for us and of our love for Him? This conviction is like the sun's rays, which cause the sap of life to flow and make the flowers of holiness blossom. This conviction is the rock on which holiness is built by serving Christ's poor and lavishing on them what we would love to do for Him in person.

If we follow this way, our faith will grow, our convic-

---

* Cf. Constitution of the International Association of Co-Workers of Mother Teresa.
** Letter, January 1973.

tion will grow, and the striving for holiness will become our daily task.

God loves those to whom He can give the most, those who expect the most from Him, who are most open to Him, those who have most need of Him and count on Him for everything.

Our works of charity are only the fruit of God's love in us. That is why those who are most united with Him love their neighbor most.

Love of Christ should be a living bond between all of us. Then the world will know that we are true missionaries of charity.

Perhaps only a smile, a little visit, or simply the fact of building a fire for someone, writing a letter for a blind person, bringing a few coals, finding a pair of shoes, reading for someone, this is only a little bit, yes, a very tiny bit, but it will be our love of God in action.

In spite of the fact that this year we might have less to show, much less in donations, if we spread and radiate love of Christ more, if we give Christ who hungers not only for bread but also our love, our presence, our contact, then 1971 could be the year of the real explosion of the love that God brings to the world.

Without God, we are human beings who have nothing to offer except sorrow and suffering.

EVERY PERSON IS UNIQUE

In serving the needs of the poor the Co-Workers should give special attention to those who are unwanted and deprived of love. For the worst disease in the world is not leprosy or tuberculosis but the feeling of being unwanted, unloved, and abandoned by everyone.

The greatest sin is the lack of love and charity, the terrible indifference to those on the fringe of the social system, who are exposed to exploitation, corruption, want, and disease. Since each member of our Society is to become a co-worker of Christ in this world of misery, each one must understand what God and the Society expect.

Let the poor, seeing the Co-Worker, be drawn to Christ and invite Him into their homes and their lives.

Let the sick and suffering find in the Co-Worker a veritable angel of comfort and consolation. And in the streets, let the little children cling to her because she reminds them of Christ who is the friend of little children.

> *When Mother Teresa, with only a few rupees in her pocket, went into the most wretched quarters of Calcutta to begin her work of love, we can imagine not only the courage it took but the tact and discretion. The people who confronted her were "hurt" individuals, unwanted, unloved, spurned or ignored by society, whose needs had to be prudently unearthed, sometimes with difficulty, because a hurt individual does not easily open up to a stranger but more likely masks his or her need behind suspicion, distrust, and outright antagonism. For this sort of work, Mother Teresa had to guard against having all the answers or quick and easy solutions.*

> *To help, without hurt to human dignity, means*
> *not only to move through the poor but to remain*
> *among them, live among them, and be a living*
> *expression of God's love.*
>
> *If Mother Teresa's efforts on behalf of the poor*
> *had come from a sense of duty, her words and her*
> *actions would not have conveyed the feeling of*
> *God's merciful love. The poor sensed the throb of*
> *her love in each of her actions. Those whom life*
> *has treated most cruelly are not deceived. They*
> *cannot be tricked or taken in by the semblance of*
> *love, by the person who shrinks from the risks of*
> *love.*
>
> *Mother Teresa was the first person who made*
> *them feel that someone really loved them and took*
> *an interest in them.*

If sometimes our poor people have had to die, it is
not because God did not take care of them but because
you and I have done nothing, have not been an instrument of love in God's hands; it is because we have
failed to recognize Him, Christ, when He came again
in the guise of distress, of a man or woman forsaken,
of a child abandoned.

Some time ago a little child came to our house about
midnight. I went down and there stood this little one
in tears. Upon questioning she said: "I went to my
mother and she did not want me; I went to my father
and he did not want me. You, do you want me?"

Here, in Melbourne, there are forlorn people who
are not loved; yet these people are God's . . . and they
are ours. In India, in Europe, wherever our Sisters

meet Christ in this pitiable disguise, it is the same hunger. Perhaps here in Australia, and in America, it is not hunger for a piece of bread or a bit of cloth to cover themselves; but there is this great loneliness, this terrible need: the feeling of being unloved, of having no one to turn to.

In Calcutta we have given refuge to more than 27,-000 persons from the street.* They come to us and we receive them, or we go out and bring them in and make them feel at home. They die so admirably . . . so admirably in the peace of God. Up to now, our Sisters and I myself have never yet seen or met a man or woman who refused to ask "pardon of God," who refused to say "I love you, my God."

We have thousands of lepers. They are so brave, so admirable, disfigured as they are. Last Christmas I went to see them and said to them that they have God's care, that God loves them specially, that they are very dear to Him and their malady is not sin.

An old man who was completely disfigured came up to me and said: "Repeat that again; it does me good. I had always heard that no one loves us. It is wonderful to know that God loves us. Say it again."

We have a Home of Mercy. We have people who have no one, who roam the streets, for whom perhaps prison and the street are the only refuge.

One of them had been seriously wounded by one of his friends. Somebody asked him: "Who did that to you?" The man began to tell all sorts of lies but would not say who did it. Later, when there was no one

---

* In 1975, more than 30,000.

around, I asked him: "Why didn't you say who wounded you?" The man looked at me and said: "His suffering would not help mine."

TRUE LOVE

On receiving the Nehru Prize, Mother Teresa underscored the importance of "true love."

Love, to be true, must first be for our neighbor. This love will bring us to God. What our Sisters, our Brothers and our Co-Workers across the world try to do is to show this love of God by deeds. To help the poor we must get to know them. Some persons who came to help us with the problems of the refugees of Bangladesh said that they had received more than they gave to those whom they had served.

This is exactly what each of us experiences when we are in contact with the poorest of the poor. This contact is what our people need. They need our hands to serve them and our hearts to love them. Think of the loneliness of old people, without means, without love, with absolutely no one to care about them. There are many places where we can see this suffering, this hunger for love, which only you and I can satisfy.

Think of forsaken children. One day I saw a little child that would not eat; her mother had died. Then I found a Sister who looked like her mother and I told her just to play with the child, and the child's appetite returned.

Responding to Prince Philip, who had presented her with the Templeton Prize, Mother Teresa said:

Dear Co-Workers, let us give thanks to God that Mr. Templeton has had the courage to dispense for God's glory the wealth he received so generously from God. Giving me this prize is giving it to all who are partners with me, across the world, in the work of love.

Here in England, how many isolated individuals there are, known only by their house number. So where do we start? Do we really know if there is someone, perhaps next door to us? Perhaps there is a blind person who would be happy if someone read the paper to him or her. Perhaps there is a wealthy individual who has no one to visit him. He has much other wealth, but he is lost in it. There is no human contact, and he needs your contact. Some time ago a very wealthy man came to us and said: "See this? I want to give it to you so that someone will come and visit us. I am half blind, and my wife is depressed; our children have left us to go abroad and we are dying of loneliness."

And in Melbourne I paid a visit to an old man no one knew existed. I saw that his room was in horrible condition and I wanted to clean it up, but he stopped me: "I'm all right." I kept quiet, and finally he let me go ahead. In his room was a beautiful lamp, covered with dust. I asked: "Why don't you light the lamp?" He replied: "What for? Nobody comes to see me, and I don't need a lamp." Then I said to him: "Will you light the lamp if the Sisters come to see you?" "Yes," he said, "if I hear a human voice, I will light it." The other day he sent me word: "Tell my friend that the lamp she lit in my life burns constantly."

These are the people we must learn to know. Knowing them will bring us to love them and to love helping them. We must not be satisfied with gifts of money. Money is not enough. Money can be got. But they need your hands to help them; they need your hearts to love them.

Very often I ask for gifts other than money. I can get these things if I want them, but I ask for them in order to get the presence of the donor, just to touch those to whom he or she gives, just to smile on them, just to give them some attention. That means so much to our people!

It is the same Jesus who met Saul on his way to Damascus to stir up trouble and kill and destroy Christians, and who said: "Saul, Saul, why do you persecute me?" And to whom Saul replied: "Who are you, Lord?" "I am Jesus whom you persecute."

And today, it is the same Christ, the same Jesus, in our poor who are unwanted. They are of no use to society, and nobody has time for them. It is you and I, if our love is true, who must seek them out.

The first time I was in London I went out at night. It was a very cold night and we met people in the street. There was a respectable old man shivering from the cold. With him was another old man, a black, who had opened his coat to wrap it around the other man against the cold. "Take me away, anywhere," the first man said to the other; "I would like to sleep between two sheets." He was a distinguished looking man who must have known better days, but there he was. And we looked around, and we saw many others.

And if there had been only one, it is Jesus. And, as Scripture says: "I looked for someone to care for me and I could find none." How terrible it would be if Jesus had to say that to us today.

Without the chance to receive the message of religious thought, even the most honest and most intelligent mind is really nothing more than a bee caught in a bottle.

I want people to get involved in the actual work we do, for their own sakes and for ours. I never ask them for money, nothing like that. I only ask them to bring their love, to bring their hands to help. Then, when they meet those in need, their first reaction is to do something for them. And when they come the second time, they already are committed. After a while, they feel that they belong to the poor; they understand their need for love, who they are, and what they themselves can do for them.

> *Love must be real. The reality of love is in the tongue that is not afraid to open up, in the offer to help that makes one vulnerable to the other, in the deed that treats the poor as equals. It says to the other, "you exist."*
>
> *Every person has the right to a minimum of goods for "security," but still more to justice, to growth, to free speech. Every person has the right to be "unique," to be an individual with human dignity.* *

* International Constitution, 6.

To humor the fancies of the poor is to begin with them from where they are, to take them by the hand so they may know they are thought of, counted on, "needed."

> *There the leper stood, straight up, in his arms a small basket of cabbage. In his arms, because on his hands not a single finger was left. He said to the Father of the lepers (Father Raoul Follereau): "I have lost my fingers and my hands, but I have kept my courage. I wanted to be someone, someone who works and sings, as you have said to us. So I learned to help myself with my hands—and without hands. A hundred times the tool fell to the ground. A hundred times I got down on my knees to pick it up. I have just brought in my first vegetables. I give them to you, because it is you who taught me that I was not an unwanted."*

We shall never know all the good that a simple smile can do.

We speak of our God, good, clement, and understanding; but are we the living proof of it? Those who suffer, can they see this goodness, this forgiving God, this real understanding in us?

Never let anyone come to you without coming away better and happier. Everyone should see goodness in your face, in your eyes, in your smile.

In the dispensaries, in the slums, wherever we are, we are the light of God's goodness.

Thoughtfulness, the kindly regard for others, is the beginning of holiness. If you learn the art of being

thoughtful, you will be more and more like Christ; His
heart was kind and gentle, and He always thought of
others. Our vocation, to be beautiful, must be full of
regard for others. Jesus did good wherever He went.
Our Lady at Cana thought only of the needs of others
and told Jesus about them.

I AM A MAN

The Co-Workers recognize the dignity, the individu-
ality, and the infinite value of every human being.*

> *Sandro Bordignon, the French journalist, says of
> Mother Teresa: "I believe that no other philoso-
> pher or humanist has such a lively sense of the
> humanity and the value of every human being.
> The presence of the mayor, the cardinal, the leper,
> or anyone of the poor, it makes no difference; she
> meets and treats them with the same respect."*
>
> *Above all else, the poor one is a person. And if
> works of charity are collective, charity itself is
> individual.*
>
> *Ladies of fashion may meet in thick-carpeted
> homes, draw up their monthly schedule of philan-
> thropies, make a financial report and see the
> slums from afar, like the tourist viewing the city
> below. This is necessary but not enough. From her
> Co-Workers Mother Teresa demands direct con-
> tact with the poor: visiting them in person, clean-
> ing their homes, dressing their wounds. Charity is*

* Constitution, 6.

*directed toward someone, toward a person. When
the poor "hit bottom," they can lose the idea that
they are human beings.*

*Father Raoul Follereau tells of a leper who
tried to take advantage of the revulsion his condition can inspire. One evening, seeing some women
alone, he went up to them and said: "Give me
money or I will touch your faces and you will be
lepers." Terrified, the women complied. Father
Raoul heard about it and gave him a tongue lash-
ing for his efforts. But the culprit had nothing to
say. Worse, there was no sign of remorse. Finally
the priest, beside himself, yelled out: "Yes or no,
are you a man?" The leper straightened up and,
his eyes glistening, said: "You are right. I did
wrong. I am a man." And because he had been
treated as a "man," he added: "Thanks."*

*To love one's neighbor the way Mother Teresa
does it is necessary to dismiss all thought of ine-
quality. She sees the face of Christ in the leper as
well as in the radiant beauty of a little child. And
she believes in the person-to-person relationship.*

What is important to us is the individual. To get to
love a person, there must be close contact. If we wait
for the numbers, we will be lost in the numbers, and
we will never be able to show that person the necessary love and respect. Every person is for me the only
person in the world at that moment.

I believe that people today think the poor are not
humans like them. They look down on them. But if

they had a deep respect for the poor, I am sure it would be easy for them to come closer to them, and to see that they have as much right to the things of life and to love as anybody has. In these times of development, everybody is in a hurry and rushing about, and on the way there are people falling down, people who do not have the strength to run. It is these that we want to help and take care of.

I never take care of crowds, only of a person. If I stopped to look at the crowds, I would never begin. Love is a fruit always in season.

> *To make herself accepted, Mother Teresa identifies with the poor. She eats the same food, wears the same clothes.*
>
> *At the Congress of 1973, in Melbourne, Mother Teresa spoke of Christ identifying Himself with the sick, the naked, the homeless, the hungry.*

Hungry, not only for bread but also to exist for someone; naked, not only for lack of clothing but also lack of compassion, since very few people have compassion for the nameless multitude; homeless, not only having no home of wood or stone but no friendly soul of whom one can say "I have someone."

Our little children are in this category of the rejected and unloved. Today the problem that troubles so many people is not only the fear that the world is becoming overpopulated, but more and more we hear it argued that Providence cannot take care of all the babies that will be born.

For my part, if abortion is permitted in countries

that lack for nothing, these countries are the poorest of the poor. I would like to open in these countries many institutions for children. We have these small institutions all over India, and up to now we have never had to refuse a single child. And, most wonderfully, God has seen to it that each of these children that escaped death at the hands of their parents has found a home with new parents.

In Calcutta, we have tried to combat abortion by adoption, and we have been able to give many little ones who were destined to die a father and a mother. For us, in India, it is a wonderful thing, because by law these children are untouchables.

As for countries that have enacted laws permitting abortion as a so-called natural act, we must pray for them, because the sin is great. It is murder.

We were invited to Bangladesh to work with girls who had been abused by soldiers. Driven by despair and disgrace, some committed suicide. We opened a Home for Children for them, and had to overcome great difficulties, as it is against Moslem and Hindu law to take back into society girls like these who have been abused.

But when Mujibu said that these girls were national heroes, that they had tried to defend their purity and had fought for their country, their own parents came to get them. There were even young men who offered to marry them.

And then, some persons were asked to perform abortions on them. It was a terrible battle. I told them that these girls had been abused, forced, and had not wanted to sin, and that what some people wanted to do to them or help them do would be an act of murder. For the rest of their lives they would never forget that as mothers they had killed their children.

The government agreed with us, and it was announced that every child for which the mother had wanted an abortion should be brought to our home. Of the forty children we have received, more than thirty have been adopted by wonderful families. This is how we try to combat abortion.

Because our Sisters work in the slums, we have found more and more young mothers dying and children born deformed, and we could not find the reason. Looking deeper, we discovered that because of their ignorance these young women were being taken advantage of and abused. So we prayed to God to send us someone who could undertake the task of helping these women face this problem with a clean conscience, a healthy body in a happy family. We were blessed with the vocation we needed, a Sister from the Maurice Islands who had taken courses on natural family planning. We have begun the work of providing information, and today we have more than three thousand families putting it into practice, with a success rate of 95–96 percent.

When people saw what was happening in their families, they came to thank us. Some said: "Our family has remained together; our family is enjoying good health and we can have a baby when we want it."

*Ralph Rolls asked Mother Teresa what she had
been able to observe in England today on this subject. She replied:*

England seems to be hesitant about protecting unborn children and apparently tries to get rid of
them. They get rid of them by killing life; and to me,
that is an obvious sign either that the country is
very poor and does not have the means to take care
of lives that God has created, or that it has somehow
been misled.

*Rolls then asked her if she preferred that abortion
be illegal.*

I do not say legal or illegal, but I think that no
human hand should be raised to kill life, since life is
God's life in us, even in an unborn child. And I think
that the cry of these children who are killed before
coming into the world must be heard by God.

*Rolls asked how society could cope with so many
children, if they all came into the world.*

Jesus said that we are much more important in the
eyes of His Father than the grass, the birds, and the
flowers of the earth. And that if He takes care of these
things, how much more He would take care of His own
life in us. He cannot deceive us. Life is God's greatest
gift to human beings, and humans are created in the
image of God. Life belongs to God and we do not have
the right to destroy it.

*Our world tends toward the absurd, says Bordig-
non. We have created conditions of life un-*

> *dreamed twenty years ago; we have increased
> many times over the capacity to produce; we have
> made unparalleled technological advances. In
> view of this, it seems madness not to be able to feed
> all the people in the world.*
>
> *We are preoccupied with the demographic ex-
> plosion and sometimes wonder what is to be
> gained by saving the newborn infants that
> Mother Teresa retrieves from the trash bins of
> Calcutta. But then says Bordignon, I saw how
> she thrilled when one of these tiny ones gave
> signs of life. "It lives!" she exclaimed, and that
> for Mother Teresa is joy.*
>
> *She was also asked about the reasons for the
> unexpected success of her natural family planning
> efforts. She replied quite simply:*

People understood the usefulness of self-control.

BULLDOZER OF CHRIST

Deep faith in action is love, and love in action is service.

> *Mother Teresa asks her Co-Workers to dedicate
> themselves to wholehearted free "service" to the
> poorest of the poor.**

I want the Co-Workers to put their hands and
hearts at the service of the people. If they do not
come in close contact with them, they cannot know
who the poor are. That is why, especially here in Cal-

* Constitution, 5.

cutta, we have a goodly number of non-Christians and Christians working together in the Home for the Dying and other places. Some groups prepare bandages and medicine for the lepers. For example, an Australian came the other day to make a large donation. But after making the donation he said: "This is something outside of myself; now I want to give something of myself." Since then, he comes regularly to the Home for the Dying to shave the sick and talk with them. He gives not only his money but also his time. He could have spent both his money and time on himself, but he wanted to spend himself instead.

Mother Teresa's service is not aimless agitation, not helter-skelter activity lost in numbers. Rather, it is centered on Jesus, a single-minded service to Jesus in the guise of the poor.

To serve, according to Mother Teresa, is to embrace and follow Christ the Servant. "I am with you as one who serves" (Luke 22:27).

To serve is to be a servant of Christ present in the world, especially in his poor. The servant of Christ practices the compassion of Christ, which does not wait for gratitude. True compassion endures failure, conflict, thanklessness.

To serve is to know and acknowledge the truth; to recognize the part that ignorance or innocence can play in those who fall; to give support rather than pass judgment; to be the voice of the voiceless; and never to yield to the temptation to be cross or unkind.

> *To serve is to go to those who cannot render service for service, who show no gratitude, to those who are bitter, who suffer from lack of a kindly look, a smile. Mother Teresa stresses the power of a smile that communicates the joy of God.*
>
> *Helping others ought to go further than the impersonal act of almsgiving. To give of our superfluity is not the same as giving of ourselves, or entering into the suffering of others.*
>
> *Being rich or poor is not always a question of material possessions. Mother Teresa points out that distress, isolation, suffering can also be the lot of those who have material wealth. To serve is to take upon one's shoulders the burdens of others, to share their fears and anxieties.*
>
> *Mother Teresa's service is a constant search for union with God. She serves God by serving others, children of God whose true worth she knows. Jesus bled for the poor. He wept.*
>
> *Mother Teresa underlines the importance of being co-workers of Christ:*

How much we ought to love our Society (the Missionaries of Charity) and show our gratitude by being what God and the Society expect of us: true co-workers of Christ. More than ever, we ought to do our work for Christ who was poor, and for the poor who are Christ's, with a humble and devoted heart.

In order to survive, love has to be nourished by sacrifices. The words of Jesus, "Love one another as I have loved you," must be not only a light to us but a flame that consumes the self in us.

Love should be as natural as living and breathing. The Little Flower said: "When I act and think charitably, I feel it is Jesus working in me; the deeper my union with him, the stronger my love for the residents of Carmel."

> *Mother Teresa's congregation has experienced an astonishing vitality. She accounts for this by saying:*

We put our hands, our eyes, our hearts at Christ's disposal so that he may act through us.

> *She has been called a "bulldozer of Christ," because nothing stops her. Everything is urgent. From Calcutta Jean Vanier writes.*
>
> *"I have just spent an hour with Mother Teresa. I was struck by her sense of urgency. She always seems to be returning from somewhere, New York, London, Rome, Gaza, the Yemen, Ethiopia, Amman. She spoke of Cambodia. Her acute sensitivity to the suffering in the world, which is almost an obsession, prods her to action. She was looking for a helicopter to bring food to the rural population of Ethiopia, and trying to find a way of helping Arabs and Israelis exchange their dead, as well as working out a plan to give assistance to the religious in Cambodia."*
>
> *She had seen the prime minister of Israel and the ruler of Gaza. She was troubled by the hatred in the hearts of Arabs and Jews. She spoke of the suffering she had seen in London, and of her Home for the Dying in Calcutta, which has never been so full.*

Could one set up a canteen at the railroad station in Saaldad for the starving?

> *Her creative talent is astonishing, always in search of solutions. Now she wants to see Madame Gandhi. Nothing is impossible. Her abandonment to God is total. Her wrinkled face shows great compassion—and fatigue; she has aged . . .*
>
> *But she is a "bulldozer of Christ." Nothing stops her. She is truly an instrument of God, and yet she is such a small woman . . .*
>
> *She does not like to speak of her community, of structures, only of the poor. One time she went to Rome for a meeting of Major Superiors and reported.*

But I said nothing. All the talk was about structures; I understood nothing. My mind was somewhere else.

> *She said this without a hint of criticism. In fact, I have never heard her make the least critical remark about anyone.*
>
> *No work is too much for Mother Teresa. Not content with washing feet, she repairs roofs damaged by the wind . . . and leads a march of seven kilometers through the streets of Milan to build solidarity with the Third World.*
>
> *She scarcely has time anymore to write to her Sisters:*

All my time is taken up by everybody; and with the Sisters it is the same. They work without interruption for the sick or the children and really do not have time to write. Tell the ailing Sisters not to be disappointed if they do not receive letters, because the work is all-consuming.*

LOVE ACCEPTS ALL AND GIVES ALL

Love and service are the key to giving.

> *"Freely have you received . . . freely give." Mother Teresa could say with one of our contemporaries: "I no longer belong to myself. Some evenings, after being worn out by others, I do not know who I am. I am someone else; I am God's."*

Love accepts all and gives all.

> *Mother Teresa's charity requires this total renunciation.*
>
> *In the constitution that governs her Co-Workers Mother Teresa declares:*

Co-Workers must recognize that all goods of this world are free gifts of God and that no one has the right to excess wealth when others are dying of hunger. Co-Workers seek to correct this grave injustice through voluntary poverty and the sacrifice of luxuries in their daily life.**

> *But Mother Teresa acknowledges that sometimes the wealthy make it a point to give.*

The wealthy, in their own way, do sometimes want to share in the misfortune of others. The pity is that

---

* Letter to Jacqueline de Decker.
** Constitution, 8.

they do not truly put themselves out. The new generation, especially the children, understand better. Children in England are making sacrifices to give a piece of bread to our children. Children of Denmark are making sacrifices to give them a glass of milk daily, and children of Germany are doing the same to give them daily vitamins. These are ways of learning to love. Children like these, when they grow up, will know what it means to give and will want to do so.

A beautiful display of "giving" is recounted by Sister Frederick. Students in a school in Canada went twenty-five hours without eating, in sympathy with those "who are starving." The pupils experienced what it means to go hungry and sent their impressions to Mother Teresa. Their only food was Christ, whom they received at a special Eucharist, celebrated at midnight.

Another class arranged a "different experience," going without sleep for twenty-five hours. Like Christ, these young people bore in their flesh the cost of giving. Perhaps, through their sacrifice, somewhere in the world starving people were fed. It was their way of sharing in the suffering of others.

We must suffer with Christ and that is why we want to share in the sufferings of the poor. Our congregation could die out in my lifetime, if the Sisters do not walk with the suffering Christ, and if the Sisters do not remain poor.

Our strict poverty is our safeguard. We do not want to begin by serving the poor and little by little end up

serving the rich, like other religious orders in history.
In order to understand and help those who lack everything, we must live like them. The difference is that
our destitute ones are poor by force of circumstance,
whereas we are by choice.

The Sisters do little things like help the children,
visit the lonely, the sick, the poorest of the poor.

In one of the houses our Sisters visited, a woman
living alone had been dead a long time before anyone
knew it, and then they found out only because her
corpse had begun to rot. Her neighbors didn't even
know her name.

When someone says to me that the Sisters do not
perform great tasks, that they do little things in their
quiet manner, I reply that if they helped only one
person, it would all be worth while.

Jesus died for one person, for one sinner.

> *Mother Teresa has no problem with culture,
> colonialism, or proselytism. When mass is cele-
> brated with her poor in the pagan temple of Kali,
> no one takes offense. Rather, the emaciated wor-
> shippers, almost drained of life—so close are they
> to death—seem suffused with a sort of holiness,
> the holiness that is the sister of suffering and is
> not of this world.*

HAVING THE EXPERIENCE OF
HAVING NOTHING

> *Mother Teresa exemplifies the call of Christ "not
> to lay up for yourselves treasures on earth, where*

> *moth and rust consume and where thieves break in and steal, but lay up for yourselves treasures in heaven, where neither moth nor rust consume and where thieves do not break in and steal" (Matthew 6:19).*
>
> *In the Old Testament the prophet Isaiah directs his maledictions against the wealthy of Jerusalem: "Woe to those who join house to house, who add field to field, until there is no more room, and you are made to dwell alone in the midst of the land . . . many houses shall be desolate, large and beautiful houses, without inhabitant" (Isaiah 5: 8–9).*
>
> *The spirit of poverty seen in the Missionaries of Charity ought to remind the world of the prophet's denunciations. A Mother Teresa is a standing rebuke to the mad pursuit of money.*
>
> *For her activities on behalf of the poor she has never accepted help from the state. She considers her work a work of Providence.*

Even in the beginning, I never asked for money. I wanted to serve the poor simply for love of God. I wanted the poor to receive free what the rich get for themselves with money.

> *She regards wealth as an evil—worse than an evil, a disaster—because it destroys generosity, closes up the heart, suffocates. When, on occasion, she appears in the homes of the rich, she has an uncomfortable feeling of suffocation. When she was invited to Washington by Senator Ted Kennedy, the British writer St. John Stevas was present and*

> *asked her how she felt in the midst of such opu-*
> *lence. She replied that she was miserable, and*
> *that she was there, in those beautiful drawing*
> *rooms of Washington, only because someone had*
> *to plead the cause of the poor.*
>
> *But she does not condemn the rich. Instead of*
> *passing judgment, she says:*

Who are we that we can judge the rich? Our task is
to bring the rich and the poor together, to be their
point of contact.

> *Mother Teresa preaches revolution, but her idea*
> *of revolution is not confrontation. Rather it is*
> *the coming together, the mutually beneficial*
> *meeting of the rich and the poor. Already she sees*
> *results:*

Upper-caste families are adopting children we res-
cue from the streets, which is indeed revolutionary,
when one remembers the prejudice of the caste system. In this coming together the rich become better,
since they demonstrate love of God to the poor, and
the poor become better through the love they receive
from the rich.

> *Mother Teresa dignifies the poor. A journalist*
> *asked her who she thought was doing most for the*
> *Gospel today: Pope John XXIII, Martin Luther*
> *King, Gandhi . . .*

I believe that the most important person in the
world today is the poor person, since he or she has the
capacity to suffer and work hard.

> *To Mother Teresa, says Bordignon, the poor person is "the prophet of a new humanity." Perhaps we still worship the god of progress too much to appreciate the promise that her words hold for humanity.*
>
> *Tender-hearted and self-effacing, Mother Teresa carries an untiring charity in her heart, on her lips, in her look, and even in the elongated fingers so accustomed to dressing wounds. A burning love impels her to follow her Lord, to recognize Him in the peeping cry of an infant, in the wailing of a lost child, in the stumps of a leper, in the poor dying in the streets. A sensitive angel of mercy, she walked through Harlem with only a rosary in her hands for protection, in a quarter where no white dared to venture alone. Back in India, she moves among the dying,*

so that they may die seeing a kindly face and know there are people who love them and want to give them, at least in their final hours, a taste of human and divine love.

> *And also that they may have the comfort of seeing this woman bend over them and share the agony in their eyes, this woman who takes away fear and gives them a glance at the same little crucifix (the one she wears) that was kissed three times by a notorious criminal before his execution—as though in answer to the unknown prayers of St. Theresa of the Child Jesus. Of the dying she says:*

They lived like animals, but here they die like angels.

> *Mother Teresa's work is immense, but in her eyes so small as to be "a drop in the ocean."*
> *This drop, however, would be missed if it were not in the ocean. But she does not consider it a glittering drop. As she says:*

We do not strive for spectacular actions. What counts is the gift of yourself, the degree of love you put into each of your deeds.

> *This drop is the little tear that Mother Teresa, aglow with divine love, gathers from the eyelid of one who is dying.*

NO LOVE WITHOUT FORGIVING, NO FORGIVING WITHOUT PEACE

> *This nun in a sari is so full of mercy that she attracts the poor because she is emptied of self in totally giving herself. She is not afraid to spend herself, to identify with her brother or sister in distress, or to launch into a career of mercy and forgiveness not counting the cost. She has met Christ in her work and teaches the lesson that we must forgive, since we have need to be forgiven.*

If we remember that we are sinners and have need of forgiveness, it is very easy to forgive others. If I did not understand that, it would be hard for me to say "I forgive you" to someone who comes to me.

> *Ralph Rolls asked if one had to be a Christian in order to forgive.*

Not at all, not at all. Every human being comes from the hand of God and we all know how much God loves us. Whatever our belief, we must learn to forgive if we want truly to love.

> *Have you any evidence of this forgiveness?*

Yes, I saw it in Belfast. Certain families I visited had lost members in the civil strife. These people forgave. They had neither hatred nor rancor toward those who had massacred their children.

> *The Missionary Brothers of Charity are doing wonderful work and having an influence on the lives of others. One young man had been a driver for a band of professional thieves. Seeing the work done by the Brothers in his neighborhood, he decided to change his way of life. He married a young woman who had been nursed back to health by the Brothers and now uses his leisure time to help them.*
>
> *It is a great thing to help build communities of love and goodness, which are signs of hope and strength. These signs may not be much in themselves, but they are filled with promise for peace and forgiveness in the world.*
>
> *In the encyclical* Pacem in Terris, *Pope John XXIII says: "Peace cannot reign among men unless it first reigns in each of them, that is, unless each observes in himself the order wanted by God."*

We must all work for peace. Before we can have this peace, we must learn from Jesus to be kind and humble of heart. Only humility can bring us to unity, and unity to peace. Therefore, let us help one another to draw so near to Jesus that we can learn with joy the lesson of humility.

Think of the oppressed countries. The greatest need in Bangladesh is for forgiveness. There is so much bitterness and hatred—you have no idea of what these poor people have suffered. If they could feel that someone cares about them, that they are loved, perhaps they would find it in their hearts to forgive. I believe that is the only thing that can bring peace.

We shall make this year a year of peace in a very special way. To this end we shall try to speak more to God and with God, and less to men and with men. Let us preach peace as Christ did. He went about doing good everywhere. He did not stop His works of charity because the Pharisees or others opposed Him and tried to destroy the work of His Father.

Cardinal Newman wrote: "Help me to spread your fragrance everywhere I go. Let me preach you without preaching, not by words but by my example; by the catching force, the sympathetic influence of what I do, the evident fullness of the love my heart bears to you."

SUFFERING AND JOYFULNESS

> *Not wanting Christ is the cause of suffering, today, in the world.*
>
> *Suffering can become a "gift," says Mother Teresa.*

Suffering in itself is nothing; but suffering that is sharing in the Passion of Christ is a wonderful gift, the most beautiful gift: a gift and proof of love, because in giving us his Son the Father showed that He loves the world. So, it proved that this was a gift, the greatest gift of love, because His suffering was the expiation for sin.

The suffering in Bangladesh is like an enormous Calvary, where the Body of Christ is crucified once more.

> *The barbarity of war scars the souls of people with a hatred that forgiveness, charity, and love alone can heal.*
>
> *In the appearance of those who have been "deformed" by suffering, Mother Teresa finds the outraged figure of Jesus: Jesus is present in those who are the despised and the outcasts of humanity. Jesus is transfixed in men and women of sorrow known only by their suffering, before whom we shield our eyes and flee.*
>
> *Classic outcasts from humanity, from whom we shrink and run away, lepers inevitably attracted the unfathomable love of Mother Teresa.*
>
> *Considerable progress has been made, however, in changing the attitude toward lepers. Leprosy is no longer seen as a disgrace but as a disease.*

At death we will not be judged by the amount of work we did but by the love we put into it. And this love must come from self-sacrifice and be felt until it hurts.

The heart of the work of the Missionaries of Charity

is committed to the four million lepers in the country. Leprosy is certainly a great evil, but not as great as being deprived of love or being unwanted or abandoned.

Lepers may be disfigured but they, like the poor, are wonderful people, with a great capacity for love.

> *Mother Teresa's love pours out on the victims of leprosy: young people and old, some of them unable to walk, reduced to crawling. She has discovered a feeling of community among them, a true comity of soul. Notwithstanding their offensive bodies, their ravaged faces, and rotting flesh, she finds in them a "hidden quality" that lends them human dignity. Working among them, she herself is so to speak transformed and becomes insensitive to the odor of the leprosarium. She forgets that she is among lepers. Appearances give way as the human person emerges. It is the person, not the leper that she knows and calls by name. She does not think of them as lepers but as individuals with their own names. Hers is a work of love, the fruit and sign of God's grace.*
>
> *Those who have seen Mother Teresa and her Sisters working in a leprosarium all testify that they are joyous and would not think of giving up this work. They love these lepers and follow them through their Calvary to the cemetery—the most pathetic funeral cortege one can imagine, behind an old rattling hearse with its plumed panels of glass.*
>
> *Pitiful scenes occur that tear at Mother Teresa's*

> *heart. A woman cared for at the leprosarium was
> told that her little girl also was leprous. The
> mother was beside herself, since she already had
> a boy in the leprosarium. The father came to see
> his family. The little girl limped toward him but
> stopped short of clasping his knees or throwing
> herself in his arms despite the overwhelming urge
> to do so. Remembering her condition, she just
> stood and stared at him. Her little body was
> diseased; her spirit, deprived of affection, died
> soon after. Occurrences like this make Mother
> Teresa say wherever she goes that the worst dis-
> ease is not leprosy but the want of affection.*
>
> *Other heart-rending scenes occur when lepers
> suffer the emotional trauma of leaving their
> homes to come to the leprosarium. One five-year-
> old in the leprosarium was there simply because
> two aunts who were leprous had caressed her
> when she was still a little child in the crib. The
> day she was taken away to the leprosarium
> brought a painful moment when she threw herself
> in the arms of her grandmother and said: "Will
> the Sisters love me like you? Will they hear my
> night prayers and tuck me into bed?"**

The sick can become close Co-Workers of a Sister or
Brother by offering their suffering for that Sister or
Brother.**

Each Sister should have a second self who prays and
suffers for her; and each can draw from this support

---

*From information supplied by the Society of Mary.
**Constitution, 19.

a new strength and their lives will be like a burning light that burns itself out for souls.

Suffering in itself is nothing, but suffering that shares in the Passion of Christ is a wonderful gift . . . and a sign of love.

How good God is to give you so much suffering and so much love. All of this is joy to me and gives me strength on account of you. It is your life of sacrifice that gives me strength.

| *To the sick and dying she says:*

Your prayers and sufferings are like a chalice into which we who are working can put, can pour, our love for the souls that we meet. For this, you are just as necessary as we; we and you, together, can do all things in Him who strengthens us.

The vocation of suffering Sisters is a beautiful thing. We are bearers of God's love. We carry in our hearts and in our souls the love of God who thirsts for souls. You can quench His thirst, you by your priceless suffering, and we by our hard work. You have known, you have tasted of, the chalice of His agony.

| *To her Sisters she says:*

Without our suffering, our work would only be social work, very good and useful, but it would not be the work of Jesus Christ. It would not be part of the Redemption. Jesus wanted to help us by sharing our life, our loneliness, our agony, our death. It was necessary that he become "one" with us in order to save us. He permits us to do the same. The afflictions of the poor, not only their material wretchedness but also their spiritual deprivation, must be redeemed and we must share their lives, because it is only by becoming "one" with them that we can save them, that is, bring God to them and bring them to God.

When suffering overtakes us, let us accept it with a smile. This is the greatest gift of God: having the courage to accept with a smile whatever He gives us and whatever He takes from us.

| *To an ailing woman she wrote:*

Very often I am near in thought to you, and I offer up your great sufferings when mine are small or trivial. When it is going very hard for you, then let your only refuge be in the Sacred Heart, and there my heart will find with you both strength and love. You want to suffer in pure love? Say rather in the love He chooses for you. How much I thank God for having given you to me. Give more and more, until you have no more to give.

My soul is heartened by the thought of having you to pray and suffer for me; I find it easier to smile. You do the suffering, we shall do the work. Together, we hold the same chalice in our hands.

> *I slept and I dreamed*
> *that life is all joy.*
> *I woke and I saw*
> *that life is all service.*
> *I served and I saw*
> *that service is joy!*
> *(Nath Tagore)*

Mother Teresa said to an itinerant troupe called "Chant of Asia": We give joy to people by serving them; you, you give it by your performance. Your work and ours complete each other. What you do by singing and dancing, we do by scrubbing and cleaning. It is beautiful to be able to give joy to people. I am sure that thanks to you many people are comforted. And this talent you have received, only riches can deprive you of it. As long as you are willing to be empty of yourself and to be filled with God, you will keep this talent. The day that we begin to grow rich we lose something and begin to die.

Riches, material or spiritual, can suffocate you if they are not used in the right way. I praise God that you have followed your calling. Remain as "empty" as possible, so that God can fill you. Even God cannot put anything into what already is full. He does not impose Himself on us. It is you who are going to fill the world with the love God has bestowed on you. The work of moral rearmament goes on, prudently and with love. The more prudent the more effective it is. You bring it to people, and it is for them to absorb it. People are not so much interested in seeing us, but they hunger and thirst for what God wants to give them through us. We serve the same Lord. All over the globe, people hunger and thirst for God's love. In your way, you satisfy this hunger by spreading joy. In our way, we give joy by putting ourselves at the service of the sick, the dying, the rejected.

To Mother Teresa, conveying this joy is impera-tive. A Sister asked if she could visit the poor.

> *Seeing the sad expression on her face, Mother Teresa said:*

Do not go. Go back to bed; we cannot meet the poor with a sad face.

> *Joy is "news" she wants to tell the world.*

In order to spread joy, it is necessary to have joy in one's family. Peace and war begin in the home. If we really want peace in the world, let us first love one another, in the family. We shall then have the joy of Christ, our strength. It is sometimes very hard to smile at one another. It is often hard for the husband to smile on his wife, or for the wife to smile on her husband.

Once I was asked if I was married; I said yes, and I added that it is sometimes hard for me to smile on Christ.

Attempts have been made to prove that God does not exist, but God is always proving that He does exist.

Joy is a net of love by which we can capture souls. God loves the person who gives with joy. Whoever gives with joy gives more. The best way to show, our gratitude to God and to people is to accept with joy. Joy can thrive in a heart burning with love.

We wait impatiently for the paradise where God is, but we have it in our power to be in paradise with Him, right now; being happy with Him means:

To love as He loves.
To help as He helps.

To give as He gives.
To serve as He serves.

HE MAKES THE CHOICE

> *Mother Teresa was twelve years old when she experienced the first call.* *

It was in Skopje, Yugoslavia. I was only twelve years old. I was living at home with my parents. We children went to a school that was not Catholic, but we also had very good priests who helped the boys and girls to follow their vocation according to God's call. It was at that time that I knew I was called to the poor.

Between the ages of twelve and eighteen I did not want to become a nun. We were a very happy family. But at eighteen I decided to leave home for the convent, and since then, forty years ago, I have never doubted for a moment that it was the right thing for me to do. It was God's will. He made the choice.

> *It was while visiting the quarters of the poorest that she experienced a second call.*

It was a call within my vocation—a second vocation. It meant leaving the Loreto convent, where I was very happy, to go into the streets and serve the poor.

In 1946 I was going to Darjeeling to make my retreat. On the train I heard the call to give up every-

*For the beginnings of Mother Teresa's call and apostolate to the poor, see Malcolm Muggeridge's interview with her in *Something Beautiful for God,* pp. 83 ff.

thing and follow Him, to go into the slums and serve Him among the poorest of the poor.

> *Years later Bordignon asked her what had prompted her. She said simply that she didn't exactly know. And then, with a deeply human smile, as though to help him understand, she added:*

Perhaps it was a force, the Spirit of God. I knew that God wanted something . . .

> *Mother Teresa explained to Malcolm Muggeridge the steps in leaving the Loreto convent.*

First I had to apply to the archbishop of Calcutta. Then, with his approval, the Mother General of the Sisters of Loreto permitted me to write to Rome. This was the normal procedure. I was a nun; I had taken my perpetual vows, and a nun must not leave her convent. I wrote to the Holy Father, Pope Pius XII, and by return mail received an answer on April 12. He permitted me to leave and to be a non-claustral nun, that is, to live the life of a religious but under obedience to the archbishop of Calcutta. That was in 1948.

I left the convent of Loreto and went first to the Sisters in Patna to get a little medical training so that I could go into the houses of the poor. Until then, I had only done teaching. Now I had to go into the homes and see the children and the sick.

> *Mother Teresa went to look for people lying in the streets. But first she needed a place to put them.*

We needed a shelter for these most forsaken individuals. To find one, I walked, and walked, until I
could walk no more. I understood then how exhausted
must be the truly poor, always having to look for a
little food, or some medicine, and everything. The
memory of the comfort I enjoyed at the convent of
Loreto then tempted me.

| *But she did not succumb.*

O God, because of my free choice and for the sake of
Your love alone I want to remain here and do what
Your will demands of me. No, I will not turn back. My
community, they are the poor. Their security is my
security; their health, my health. My home is to be
with the poor, no, not the poor, but the poorest among
the poorest: those who are shunned because they are
infected and filthy, full of germs and crawling with
vermin; those who do not go out to beg because they
cannot go out naked; those who do not eat because they
no longer have the strength; those who fall exhausted
to the street knowing they will die, and whom the living go out of their way to avoid; those who no longer
weep because they have run out of tears; the untouchables! The Lord wants me where I am. He will find a
solution.

| *The first Sister to enter Mother Teresa's congrega-*
| *tion was warned:*

You will have to renounce yourself. Your life will
require constant self-denial.

| *Think it over she did, but Sister Agnes became the*
| *first Missionary of Charity. Since then, vocations*

> *have never stopped coming. Mother Teresa sees*
> *this as a sign of God's favor.*

If God gives vocations, it is a sign that He wants us to go out to the poor.

> *Mother Teresa is now sure that this work is God's*
> *work and that it will continue because:*

It is His, and not mine. That is why I have no fear. I know that if the work was mine, it would die with me. But I know that it is His work, that it will endure and do much good.

> *Does she miss the comforts of Loreto, Bordignon*
> *wanted to know.*

I was the happiest Sister in that community. And it was a great sacrifice to leave the work I was doing there, but I did not leave the religious life. The change was only in the work, since the Sisters there only taught, which is an apostolate for Christ.

But my vocation, within the vocation, was for the poorest of the poor.

> *Asked why there are so few vocations in the world,*
> *she replied:*

There is too much affluence, too much comfort, a very high standard of living, not only in families but even in the religious life.

From all parts of the world young women come to India and lead a very poor life, poorer than ours, driven by the desire to get away from their environment of riches. I believe that they really want to be a living example of the poverty of Christ. It is not

enough to know the spirit of poverty; it is necessary
to know poverty itself, where one literally has nothing. Today, people, even among those who come from
a "good" environment, want to experience what "not
having" means. The majority of vocations we have
had from Europe or America asked to join our congregation, not for the work but for love of poverty.

> *One word sums up Mother Teresa: love. With the
> Little Flower she could say: I realized that love
> embodies all vocations, that love is everything,
> that it embraces all times and all places; in a
> word, that it is eternal.*

> *We do not pretend to have exhausted our subject
> —Mother Teresa and her work are not so easily
> summarized. To readers who have been touched
> by what they found in these pages, by Mother
> Teresa's appeal and example, to them we suggest
> that the best way to learn still more about her is
> by lending her not only their hearts but, in what-
> ever way practical, a helping hand. This, among
> other things, is what we have tried to put across.
> —Editors*

> *"I am an optimist, and I am convinced that as
> long as there are persons like Mother Teresa, hu-
> manity can feel justified in its hope."—GIRI, Presi-
> dent of India*

PART III

Mother Teresa Speaks to Her Religious

Delhi
20 September 1959

My Dear Sisters,

The seventh of October is a day of thanksgiving in our Society. It is the day when the Good God erected our little Society into being.

As the Society is the sole property of Our Lady, it was only right that on her great day she would grant us the grace of living and growing. It is for us to grow into a straight, beautiful, fruitful tree. Promise her that you will be a source of joy for her, just as she is the cause of our joy.

My dear children, there is so much in my heart to tell you but these two things are uppermost: charity and obedience. Be true co-workers of Christ; radiate and live His life. Be an angel of comfort to the sick, a friend to the little ones and love each other as God loves each of you with a special, most intense love. Be kind to each other. I prefer you to make mistakes in kindness than work miracles in unkindness.

Be kind in your words. See what the kindness and discretion of Our Lady brought to her. She never uttered a word of the angel's message to Joseph, and then God Himself intervened. She kept all things in her heart.

Try to excel in obedience. Now that we have three local Superiors, help them by your cheerful and prompt, blind and simple obedience. You may be more talented, more capable, better in many ways, even more holy, than your Superior. All these qualities are not required for you to obey. There is only one thing to remember: "She takes the place of God for you."

Be not blind, my children. The good God has given you His work. He wants you to do His work in His way. Failure or success mean nothing to Him, as long as you do His work according to His plan and His will. You are infallible when you obey. The devil tries his best to spoil the work of God and as he cannot do it directly to Him, he makes us do God's work in our way and this is where the devil gains and we lose.

In all our houses and in the noviciate God is blessing the generosity of the Sisters. Keep up this generosity. You have every reason to be happy. Keep smiling at Jesus in your Superiors, Sisters, and in your poor.

I must put all my energy into doing God's work well. 'I will,' said John Berchmans, Stanislaus, Margaret Mary and they did become saints.

What is a saint but a resolute soul, a soul that uses power plus action. Was not this what St. Paul meant when he said, "I can do all things in Him who strengthens me"?

With you, my Sisters, I will not be satisfied with your being just a good religious. I want you to be able to offer God a perfect sacrifice. Only holiness perfects the gift.

To resolve to be a saint costs much. Renunciation, temptation, struggles, persecutions and all kinds of sacrifices surround the resolute soul. One can love God only at one's own expense.

"I will be a saint" means: I will despoil myself of all that is not God; I will strip my heart and empty it of all artificial things; I will live in poverty and detachment. I will renounce my will, my inclinations, my whims, and fancies and make myself a willing slave to the will of God.

First Friday in November 1960

My Dearest Sisters,

On the 25th at 5:45 AM I am leaving by Pan Am and will be in America on the 26th at 6:30 AM. I go, but my heart and my mind and the whole of me is with you. It is the will of God that I should go, so let us therefore be happy. During my absence, Sister Mary Agnes, the Assistant General and the Council General will take all responsibility. God will take care of you all, if you remain one. Cling to the Society because in the center is Jesus.

I am not afraid to leave you, for I know the great gift God has given me in giving you to me. On my way back, that will be about the 15th of November, I shall go to Rome. I am going to try and see our Holy Father and beg him to grant us pontifical recognition. We are not worthy of this great gift, but if it is God's Holy will, we will get it.

During this time it would make me very happy if the seniors make sacrifices in obedience; juniors in charity; novices in poverty; and postulants in chastity.

Seniors:	obedience that is prompt, simple, blind, cheerful; for Jesus was obedient unto death.
Juniors:	charity in words, deeds, thoughts, desires, feelings; for Jesus went about doing good.
Novices:	poverty in desires and attachments, in likes and dislikes; for Jesus, being rich, made Himself poor for us.
Postulants:	chastity in thoughts and affections, in desires and attachments, in not listening to idle conversation; for Jesus is a jealous lover.

Be faithful in little things, for in them our strength lies. To the good God nothing is little because He is great and we so small. That is why He stoops down and takes the trouble to make those little things to give us a chance to prove our love for Him. Because He makes them, they are very great. He cannot make anything small; they are infinite.

To the feet of Christ's vicar on earth I will carry each of you, and I am sure with his fatherly love he will bless each one of you.

First Friday in January 1961

My Own Dearest Children,

Fidelity to the rule is the most precious and delicate flower of love we religious can give to Almighty God. The rule is the expression of the will of God—we must submit to it everywhere and always, down to the last breath.

We must be convinced that the slightest unjustified violation wounds the heart of Jesus and stains our conscience. When the rule becomes one of our greatest loves, then this love expends itself in free and joyful service.

Submission for someone who is in love is more than a duty. This is the secret of the saints.

Fidelity in the least things, not for their own sake; for this is the work of small minds, but for the sake of the great thing, which is the will of God and which I respect greatly in little things.

St. Augustine says: "Little things are indeed little, but to be faithful in little things is a great thing." Is not Our Lord equally the same in a small host as in a great one? The smallest rule contains the will of God as much as the big things of life. To be able to understand this truth I must have faith in the rule, that it is of divine origin. I must cling to the rule as a child clings to its mother. I must love the rule with my will and reason.

It does not matter that the rule often seems unnatural, hard and austere . . . . God has been so very wonderful to us and it is our duty to be very wonderful to God.

First Friday in February 1961

My Dearest Sisters,

We all want to do something beautiful for God. ... Try to imagine all kinds of sacrifices and mortifications. Take your rules and try to live them with greater love for Jesus and with Jesus.

St. Vincent compares the rules to "wings to fly to God." A dying Sister asked: "What should have I done to be a saint?" The priest answered: "Are you not familiar with this wonderful little book, your rule? If you had lived this rule you would have been a saint."

"Just think" says St. Alphonsus, "by the discharge of your duties you may become a saint."

St. Vincent says: "Keep your rules and you will become a saint, for they are holy in themselves, they also can make you holy."

St. Francis de Sales writes: "Walk on always in the punctual observance of your rules, and you will be blessed by God, for He Himself will lead you with great care." In the observance of the rule, you will find strength for the purity of conscience, fervor to fill your soul, and love that will inflame your heart.

Bauthier says: "The rule is to our will what the arteries are to our blood."

22 April 1961

My Dearest Sisters,

When you go to heaven, Our Lord is not going to ask you, "Was your Superior holy, clever, understanding, cheerful, and so forth?" but only one thing, "Did you obey me?" What a wasted life is ours if it is so full of self instead of Him, your spouse whose place she takes. If you cannot see Jesus in your Superior how will you see Jesus in the poor? How will you find Jesus in His distressing disguise? How will you love Jesus you cannot see, if you do not love your Superior whom you can see? When the devil is angry with the work of love of God and does not know how to spoil it, he will try to spoil the instruments and so indirectly spoil the work of God. Do not allow yourselves to be deceived. Obey fully, obey because you love Jesus. Obey, obey. It does not matter who they are and what they are, as long as they are He for whose sake you obey.

See how Our Lady obeyed the angel: "Be it done to me according to Thy word." Whose word? The angel's, because he took the place of God. She, the Queen of Heaven, obeys the angel. See how she obeyed St. Joseph. To her, St. Joseph was He whose place he took.

First Friday in June 1961

My Dearest Sisters,

Do not imagine that love to be true must be extraordinary. No, what we need in our love is the continuity to love the One we love. See how a lamp burns, by the continual consumption of the little drops of oil. If there are no more of these drops in the lamp, there will be no light, and the Bridegroom has a right to say: "I do not know you."

My children, what are these drops of oil in our lamps? They are the little things of everyday life: fidelity, punctuality, little words of kindness, just a little thought for others, those little acts of silence, of look and thought, of word and deed. These are the very drops of love that make our religious life burn with so much light.

Do not search for Jesus in far off lands; He is not there. He is in you. Just keep the lamp burning and you will always see Him.

First Friday in July 1961

My Dearest Sisters,

I did feel very happy to be able to give the Sacred Heart a new tabernacle in Asansol as a token of gratitude to Rev. Fr. C. Van Exem. . . . Without our suffering, our work would be just social work, very good and helpful, but it would not be the work of Jesus Christ. Jesus Christ wanted to help by sharing our life, our loneliness, our agony and death, and all that in the darkest night. . . .

All the desolation of the poor people, their material poverty, their spiritual destitution might be redeemed by our sharing it, by our being one with them, by bringing God into their lives and bringing them to God.

First Friday in August 1961

My Dearest Children,

. . . How great is our calling. How fortunate people would think themselves if they were given a chance to give personal service to the King of this world. And here we are—we can touch, serve, love Christ all the days of our lives . . .

Your work for the poor will be done better if you know the way God wants you to do it and you will know this only through obedience. Cling to your Superiors as the creeper clings. The creeper can live and grow only if it clings on something. You also will grow and live in holiness only if you cling to obedience.

First Friday in June 1962

My Dearest Children,

One day St. Margaret Mary asked Jesus: "Lord, what will Thou have me to do?"

"Give me a free hand," Jesus answered.

Let Him empty and transform you and afterwards fill the chalice of your hearts to the brim, that you in your turn, may give of your abundance. Seek Him. Knowledge will make you strong as death. Love Him trustfully without looking back, without fear. Believe that Jesus and Jesus alone is life. Serve Jesus, casting aside and forgetting all that troubles or worries you, make loved the love that is not loved.

Mother House
4 August 1962

My Dearest Children,

Let us beg Our Lady to make our hearts "meek and humble" like her Son's was. It was from her and in her that the heart of Jesus was formed. We learn humility through accepting humiliation cheerfully. We have been created for greater things; why stoop down to things that will spoil the beauty of our hearts? How

much we can learn from Our Lady! She made use of
the Almighty Power that was in her. Tell Our Lady to
tell Jesus "They have no wine," the wine of humility
and meekness, of kindness, of sweetness. . . .

                          First Friday in November 1962
My Dearest Children,
    The first lesson of the heart of Jesus is our examina-
tion of conscience. "Know thyself." Examen is a part-
nership between us and Jesus. We should not rest in
useless looks at our own miseries, but should lift our
hearts to God and His light. . . .
    . . . In our vow of obedience, is there no lessening of
our faith, seeing the human limitations of our Superior?
    Our obedience, by being prompt, simple, and cheer-
ful, is the proof of our faith. If God loves a cheerful
giver how much more would He not love an obedient
giver. . . . Obey as Christ obeyed. . . . He saw the will
of His Father—in everything and everybody—so He
could say "I do the things that are pleasing to Him."
He obeyed Caiaphas and Pilate because authority was
given from "above." He submitted to them with obedience and dignity. He did not look at the human limitations of Caiaphas and Pilate.

                                      Mother House
                                      19 May 1963
My Dearest Children,
    The greatness of Our Lady was in her humility. No
wonder Jesus, who lived so close to her, seemed to be

so anxious that we learn from Him and her but one lesson—to be meek and humble of heart.

Humility is truth, therefore in all sincerity we must be able to look up and say: "I can do all things in Him who strengthens me." By yourself you can do nothing, have nothing but sin, weakness and misery. All the gifts of nature and grace, you have them from God. . . . Why allow temptations against your vocation?

10 November 1963

My Dearest Children,

This year we must prepare a better crib, a crib of poverty. It will be easy to fill the emptiness of the crib with charity.

We think we know ourselves enough. Our very lives are all for God, therefore why spend so much time on our spiritual life? It is not that we do not make our examen; no, we do it but do it alone. We have to do it with Christ if we want to make it real. Jesus is our co-worker.

Our souls should be like a clear glass through which God can be seen. Often this glass becomes spotted with dust and dirt. To remove this dirt and dust we make our examen, so that we become once more "clean of heart." He can, and He will help us to remove the "dirt and dust" if we allow Him to do it, with a sincere will to let Him have His way. Perhaps something has been lacking in us. Our vows, our duties, the virtues, our attitude to and our contacts with our neighbors . . . provide us with food enough for reflection. If we examine ourselves and find nothing to engage our attention, we need Jesus to help us detect our infidelities.

Our examen is after all the mirror we hold up to our nature, a poor weak human nature, no doubt, but one that needs the mirror to reflect faithfully all its deficiencies. If we undertake this work more sincerely, perhaps we shall find what we thought were stumbling blocks transformed by Him into stepping stones.

February 1964

My Dearest Children,

Our life has all the more need of humility since it is so much in the public eye. People surround us with love to guarantee the fruitfulness of our works of charity. It is beautiful to see the humility of Christ "who being in the form of God, thought it not only robbery to be equal with God, but emptied Himself, taking the form of a servant being made in the likeness of man and found in habit as a man."

. . . People do not want proud Sisters, for they are like a heavy instrument in the hands of God. The poor too want to be treated like children of God, not like slaves. . . .

It is a great virtue to practice humility without our knowing that we are humble.

March 1964

My Dearest Children,

. . . There is only one true prayer, only one substantial prayer: Christ Himself. There is only one voice

that rises above the face of the earth: the voice of
Christ. . . .

3 June 1964

My Dearest Children,

. . . It is said that humility is truth and Jesus is the
Truth, therefore the one way that will make us most
Christlike is humility. Do not think that hiding your
gifts of God is the sign of humility. No, do and use
whatever gifts God has given you.

Mother House
15 August 1964

My Dearest Sisters,

Today will be one of the most beautiful feasts of Our
Lady. She fulfills her role as cause of our joy. Do we
really know why we love Our Lady so much? Because
she was the spotless mirror of God's love. . . . Are we
afraid of sin? . . . How terrible sin must be, if it has the
power to kill God's life in us, for mortal sin kills, it
causes a mortal wound in the heart of God in us. Let
us die rather than ever wound God mortally.

If venial sin is deliberately allowed to become a
daily bread, it causes moral anemia and the spiritual
life begins to crumble and fall apart. . . .

Claude de La Colombière writes: "We see after
one, two or three years, that the cowards are still
cowardly, the irregular are still irregular, the angry
ones have acquired no gentleness, the proud no humility, the lazy no fervor, the selfish no detachment

from selfishness; that communities that ought to be
fiery furnaces, where they would unceasingly burn
for love of God and where the soul would become so
Christlike, so near to God, remain frightfully medio-
cre."

Mother House
1 November 1964

My Dearest Children,

I come again and again to the same point: silence
and charity. Silence of the tongue will teach us so
much, to speak to Christ. Silence of the eyes will always help us to see God. Our eyes are like two windows through which Christ or the world comes to our
hearts? Often we need great courage to keep them
closed. . . .

The silence of the heart, like Our Lady kept all
these things in her heart.

Mother House
15 February 1965

My Dearest Sisters,

We who are wedded to Christ cannot allow any
other love into our hearts without drawing down
God's displeasure upon ourselves. God has chosen us.
He also has the right to stop choosing us, but He will
never do it of His own accord except when we force
Him to do it.

. . . Do not play with your vocation, for when you
want to preserve it, you will not find the courage to do
so. Why do we have so many broken homes? Because

of uncontrolled affections, wanting to have all the pleasures, two loves.

. . . When we left home to enter the religious life, our parents made great sacrifices to let us go and when we are unfaithful to our vocation it grieves them deeply.

"I would be happy today if her coffin had left this house," the family of a Sister who had left told me.

Mother House
27 June 1965

My Dearest Children,

The fruit of our union with Christ is the vow of charity, just as the child is the fruit of the sacrament of matrimony. . . . Just as the lamp cannot burn without oil, so the vow of charity cannot live without the vows of poverty and obedience. . . .

San Felipe
6 August 1965

My Dearest Children, Sisters and Brothers,

From Our Lady we will ask for a delicate love for God's poor. . . . Here we have real spiritual slums. . . .

Cocorote
5 July 1966

My Dearest Sisters,

. . . Smiling novices, I can hear the music of your laughter of joy right here in Venezuela.

Zealous young professed, the sound of your footsteps in search of souls must be like a sweet music for Jesus. Humble students, keep this Light of Christ, the lamp burning across your books, ever full of oil, so that you may become a true light of Christ in the slums.

Waltair
31 October 1966

My Dearest Children,

It is our emptiness and lowliness that God needs and not our plenitude. These are a few of the ways we can practice humility:

Speak as little as possible of oneself.
Mind one's own business.
Avoid curiosity.
Do not want to manage other people's affairs.
Accept contradiction and correction cheerfully.
Pass over the mistakes of others.
Accept blame when innocent.
Yield to the will of others.
Accept insults and injuries.
Accept being slighted, forgotten, and disliked.
Be kind and gentle even under provocation.
Do not seek to be specially loved and admired.
Never stand on one's dignity.
Yield in discussion even though one is right.
Choose always the hardest.

Mother House
13 June 1967

My Dearest Sisters,

Make it a special point to become God's sign in your community. We must radiate the joy of being poor but do not speak about it. Just be happy to be poor with Christ. . . .

Air India Across the Ocean
17 September 1967

My Dearest Children,

Once again I am crossing the ocean to prepare the way for you in search of God's poor.

Don Marmion says: "All you have to do is to leave yourself absolutely in His hands, like wax, for He cuts away mercilessly all the unnecessary parts." And when temptation to leave the order came to him he prostrated himself before the tabernacle and cried out: "Let me be cut to pieces rather than leave the monastery."

Are we strong enough to prefer being cut to pieces rather than give up Christ?

We do not change our profession as we change our clothes. Nowadays everything is getting looser and looser. People are trying to loosen the most sacred bindings. Are we to be guided by them or will we cling to the rock, Christ? . . .

Mother House
12 April 1968

My Dearest Children,

. . . Work without love is a slavery. The church wants "renewal." Renewal does not mean the changing of habit and a few prayers. A renewal should be faithfulness to the spirit of the Constitutions.

Mother House
18 May 1968

My Dearest Children,

We must feel the suffering of our people. To be transfigured we have to be disfigured in our own sight.

Mother House
18 July 1968

My Dearest Children,

Offer to God every word you say, every movement you make. We must more and more fall in love with God. Let it not be said that one single woman in the whole world loves her husband better than we do Christ.

Mother House
28 January 1969

My Dearest Superiors and Sisters,

See the compassion of Christ toward Judas. The Master who kept the "sacred silence" would not betray him to his companions. Jesus could have easily spoken in public and told the hidden intentions and deeds of Judas. Rather He showed mercy instead of condemning him. He called "Friend" and if Judas would have only looked into the eyes of Jesus, today Judas would have been the friend of God's mercy.

Mother House
7 May 1969

My Dearest Sisters,

These are very difficult times in the church. Do not get mixed up in gossip conversations. You hear of priests and nuns leaving and of many broken homes, but do not forget there are thousands and thousands of priests and nuns and happy families faithful unto death. This trial will purify the church of her human infirmities and she will come out of it beautiful and true.

Mother House
25 November 1969

My Dearest Children,

Next week we begin with the church the season of Advent. It is like springtime. He comes like a little child so much in need of His mother. Let us see and touch the greatness that fills the depths of their humility, Jesus' and Mary's. If we really want God to fill us we must empty ourselves through humility of all that is selfishness in us.

Mother House
19 February 1970

My Dearest Children,

The first week of Lent is nearly over. He still keeps looking for "one" to console Him. Do you try to be that "one"? Today Christ, in His vicar and the church, is being humiliated through pride in acts of disobedience and disloyalty, scourged by evil tongues.

He is thirsty for the kindness He begs from you, naked for the loyalty He hopes of you.

Today much of the suffering in the church and outside of it is caused solely by misunderstood notions of freedom and renewal. We cannot be free unless we are able to surrender our will freely to the will of God. We cannot renew unless we have the humility and the courage to acknowledge what is to be renewed in us. Therefore, be careful of people who come to you with wonderful speeches on freedom and renewal; they actually deceive and take away from you the joy and peace of Christ, the Life.

Mother House
14 March 1970

My Dearest Children,

Calcutta is really sharing in the Passion of Christ. It is sad to see so much sorrow in our beloved Calcutta. But just like Christ who after the Passion rose to live forever, so Calcutta will rise again and be the Mother of the Poor. . . . Shanti Nagar is really growing into a beautiful Town of Peace. . . .

Plane to New York
11 October 1970

My Dearest Children,

. . . Instead of spending their days in fear and trembling, our Sisters in Amman prayed the rosary continuously and the result was that on the ninth day the troops stopped near our place—peace has been proclaimed. . . .

. . . Today in the words of our Holy Father every Missionary of Charity must be able "to cleanse what is dark." . . .

Mother House
17 January 1971

My Dearest Children,

. . . The award* was most unexpected and so I had no chance to let you know in time as I knew only on the 23rd when I returned from Amman.

. . . Jesus wants to live the Truth in us and through us. . . . Speak the truth, think the truth, act the truth with God, with His church, with each other and with yourselves. Do not be surprised at each other's failure. . . . Try to see and accept that every Sister is a branch in Christ the Vine. The same life-giving sap that flows from the Vine (Jesus) through each of the branches (Sisters) is the same.

*The Pope John XXIII Peace Prize.

7 March 1971

My Dearest Children,

Sacrifice, to be real, must empty us of self. We often pray "Let me share with you Your pain" and yet when a little spittle or thorn of thoughtlessness is given to us, how we forget that this is the time to share with Him His shame and pain.

If we could but remember that it is Jesus who gives us the chance through that certain person or circumstance to do something beautiful for His Father.

Superiors: try to look and see Jesus in your Sisters. Your Sisters are His in a special way because He has chosen them and given them to you to take care of and lead them through holiness to His heart. Love them as you love Christ.

Sisters: look up and see Jesus in your Superiors. Your superior is the vine and you are a branch, and unless you and they are one and allow His Father, the Gardner, to prune you, through suffering and trials, through bearing each other's burdens, neither of you will be able to bring any fruit.

The tenth of September will be the twenty-fifth anniversary of our Society. You could not show deeper gratitude than by thinking and speaking of the goodness of each other—appreciating the good your Sisters are doing, accepting each other as you are and always meeting each other with a smile.

Mother House
29 April 1971

My Dearest Children,

The news of Bangladesh seems to become worse day by day. Hatred and selfishness are destroying a whole nation.

Today when our people are being tortured and suffer untold pain, let us reflect and avoid anything that may cause deep wounds in the hearts of the poor.

We have no right to use what belongs to the poor. We eat nothing in the houses of the rich so as to be able to tell the poor when they offer us a drink: "We do not take anything outside . . ."

They love to see the Sisters in the company of Mary, rosary in hand, always making haste to bring the good news.

10 August 1971

My Dearest Children,

. . . May our Mother be a mother to each one of us and so the cause of our joy. And may each one of us be Jesus to her and so become the cause of her joy. No one learned the lesson of humility as well as Mary did. She was the handmaiden. To be a handmaiden is to be at someone's disposal—to be used according to someone's wish—with full trust and joy. Cheerfulness and joy were Our Lady's strength. Only joy could have given her the strength to go in haste over the hills of Judea to do the work of handmaiden to her cousin. So let us go in haste over the hills of difficulties.

Franciscan Handmaids of Mary Convent
15 West 124th Street, New York
15 October 1971

My Dearest Children,

The Negro Sisters have given us a separate part of their building and this will be our convent with a lovely chapel. . . .

The news of Calcutta's cyclone is so hard to accept. Our poor people are becoming poorer day by day. Be kind to them, be a comfort to the poor and take every trouble to help them. Open your eyes to the needs of the poor.

P.S. (By Sister Andrea).—The prize our Mother received was a big heavy glass vase with a silver foot and these words engraved on it:

"The Great Seraph RAPHAEL, Mightiest of Angels, Patron of Science and Healing, whose hand stirred the waters of the Pool at Bethsaida, Protector of the Young Tobias, Helper of the Patriarch Abraham, Paragon of Knowledge and Love.

To Mother Teresa, whose struggles have shaped Something Beautiful for God.

1971 Kennedy International Award."

Mother House
3 December 1971

My Dearest Children,

Love begins at home. Do not be afraid to love until it hurts.

Love your Superiors. The Society will be what you

together with your Superior make it: a fervent or a tepid, a fruitful or a dry branch.

Mother House
26 February 1972

My Dearest Children,

We have been asked by the government of Bangladesh to take care of the girls who have been misused. I want to draw your attention to the sentence Mujibur Rahman said on behalf of these girls: "They will be treated as heroines of the country because they suffered so much to protect their purity." These girls, Hindu and Muslim, out of their natural love for purity fought to protect themselves. Many committed suicide rather than lose the beautiful virtue of womanhood.

We religious who have a chance to consecrate that beautiful gift to God in loving Him with undivided love, do we really take all the trouble to protect it and make it grow in beauty and strength?

. . . During this Lenten season we will take as a special point: Forgiveness. If we do not forgive then it is a sign that we have not been forgiven.

Sister M. Francis Xavier met with a terrible car accident but thank God, as she says: "Our Lady took care of me." She was saying the rosary and had the rosary in hand when she gained consciousness.

Mother House
19 March 1972

My Dearest Children,

Today when everything is questioned and changed,
let us go back to Nazareth. How strange that Jesus
should spend thirty years doing nothing, wasting His
time, not giving His personality or His gifts a chance!
We know that at the age of twelve He silenced the
learned priests of the Temple, who knew so much and
so well. Then for thirty years we hear no more of Him.
No wonder the people were surprised when He came
in public to preach; He was known only as a carpen-
ter's son.

We hear so much of "personality," of "maturity,"
of "maternalism," and so forth, . . . and yet the
Gospel is so full of words such as "little children"
used by Jesus when addressing His grown-up apostles.

Mother House
28 June 1972

My Dearest Children,

Let us ask the Sacred Heart for one very special
grace: love for Our Lady. Ask Him to give and deepen
our love and make it more personal and intimate for
her:

To love her as He loved her.
To be a cause of joy to her as He was.
To keep close to her as He kept.
To share with her everything, even the cross.

Each one of us has our cross to bear, for this is the sign that we are His. Therefore we need her to share it with us. . . .

. . . Holiness is not a luxury but a simple duty for you and me. Very great holiness becomes very simple if we belong fully to Our Lady. . . .

. . . I am sure each one of us has much to thank God:

For all the tiring journeys we have made by road, by train, by plane, by cycle in search of souls.
For all the joy we have tried to spread throughout the world.
For letting us give Our Lady full liberty to use us.

Mother House
15 August 1972

My Dearest Children,

This is my feastday greeting to each one of you: that you may know each other at the breaking of bread and love each other in the eating of this Bread of Life.

When communicating with Christ in your heart during the partaking of the Living Bread, remember what Our Lady must have felt when the Holy Spirit overpowered her and she became full with the Body of Christ. The Spirit in her was so strong that immediately she "rose in haste" to go and serve.

At the breaking of bread they recognized Him. Do I recognize the beauty of my Sisters, the spouses of Christ? Our Lady was full of God because she lived for God alone, and yet she thought of herself only as the handmaiden of the Lord. Let us do the same.

Mother House
13 December 1972

My Dearest Children,

Let us all be very much aware of the responsibility we must share together in building up our Society as a living and fruitful branch of the Body of Christ. . . .

Jesus has warned us already: "Woe to the world because of scandals. For it must needs be that scandals come; but nevertheless woe to the one by whom the scandal comes" (Matthew 18:7).

Woe to her through whom scandals are made, wrong attitudes and worldliness being very much contrary to the poverty and obedience of Christ we have chosen. It would be a shame for us to be richer than Christ, Who being rich became poor and was "subject to them."

August 1973

My Dearest Children,

I wish you the joy of Our Lady, who because she was humble of heart could hold Jesus for nine months in her bosom. What a long Holy Communion!

Rome
24 October 1973

My Dearest Children,

So many of our Sisters' parents, brothers and sisters have gone home to God during these years. I am sure they are making a new group of Co-Workers in Heaven. . . .

. . . In Ostia, there is a terrible poverty, not hunger for food but for God. People are starving for the knowledge of God.

In Yemen, our Sisters have their hands full in spite of not yet knowing the language. One of the government officials wrote: "A new era of light and love has started in Yemen."

Mother House
14 December 1973

My Dearest Children,

Our Holy Father has proclaimed the Holy Year as Year of Reconciliation. Reconciliation begins not first with others but with ourselves. It starts by having a clean heart within. A clean heart is able to see God in others. The tongue, the part of our body that comes in such close contact with the Body of Christ can become an instrument of peace and joy or of sorrow and pain. . . . Forgive and ask to be forgiven; excuse rather than accuse. . . .

25 February 1974

My Dearest Children,

Our lives should be more and more pervaded by a profound faith in Jesus, the Bread of Life, which we should partake of with and for the poor. . . .

The Sisters assure you all of their overflowing love: from Yemen, Ostia, Addis Ababa, Lima, Gaza, Coimbatore, Vijayawada, Shivpur, Tiljala, Takda, all the new homes send you their prayers. . . .

Are we truly attempting to be the poorest of the poor? In poverty which is liberty, charity increases.

Easter, 1974

My Dearest Children,

Jesus has chosen each and every one of you to be His love and His light in the world. . . .

The spirit of sacrifice will always be the salt of our Society. . . .

PART IV

Living with the Poor and Like the Poor

Mother Teresa's Commentary on the Constitution of the Missionaries of Charity (Unpublished Documents)

"I thirst," Jesus said on the Cross. He spoke of His thirst not for water but for love.

Our aim is to quench this infinite thirst of God made man.

So the Sisters, using the four vows of chastity, poverty, obedience and wholehearted free service to the poorest of the poor, ceaselessly quench that thirsting of God.

"Nothing common" wrote St. Ignatius to the scholastics, "can satisfy the obligations by which you have bound yourselves to striving after perfection. Consider your vocation, of what character it is, and you will see what might be satisfactory in others is not so in your case."

Let us remember the words of St. Theresa of Lisieux: "How shall I show my love, since love shows itself by deeds?" Well, the little child Theresa will strew flowers: "I will let no tiny sacrifice pass, no look, no word. I wish to profit by the smallest actions and to do them for love. . . . I will sing always even if my roses must be gathered from amidst thorns and the longer and sharper the thorns, the sweeter shall be my song."

"Our Lord," she said, "has need of our love; He has no need of our works."

The same God who declares that He has no need to tell us if He be hungry did not disdain to beg a little water from the Samaritan woman. He was thirsty, but when He said "Give me to drink," He, the Creator of the Universe, was asking for the love of His creatures.

To become a saint, one must suffer much. Suffering begets love . . . and life among the souls.

For us, the carriers of God's love, how full of love we must be in order to be true to our name.

Let us always remain with Mary our Mother near our crucified Jesus, with our chalice made of the four vows and filled with the wine of self-sacrifice.

All our actions, therefore, must tend to advance our own and our neighbor's perfection by nursing the sick and dying, by gathering and teaching little street children, by visiting and caring for beggars and their children, and by giving shelter to the abandoned.

To labor at the conversion and sanctification of the poor in the slums means hard ceaseless toil, without counting the results or the cost.

To convert is to bring to God. To sanctify is to fill with God. To convert and sanctify is the work of God, but God has chosen in His great mercy the Missionaries of Charity to help Him in His own work. It is a special grace granted to the Missionaries of Charity with no merit on their part to carry the light of Christ into the dark holes and slums.

Those, therefore, who join the Institute are resolved to spend themselves unremittingly in seeking out in towns and villages, even amid squalid surroundings, the poor, the abandoned, the sick, the infirm, the dying.

Zeal for souls is the effect and the proof of true love of God. We cannot but be consumed with the desire for saving souls. Zeal is the test of love and the test of zeal is devotedness to His cause, spending life and energy in the work of souls. . . .

It cannot be denied that the active life is full of dangers, because of the numerous occasions of sin to which it gives rise, but let us be sure of God's special protection in all our works assumed under obedience. To hesitate when obedience calls us to action would be to deserve the rebuke Peter merited, "O thou of little faith, why didst thou doubt . . ."

Our Lady arose and went with haste to the hill country . . . and Mary remained about three months to do the work of a servant for her old cousin. . . . We must possess before we can give. She who has the mission to distribute must first increase in the knowledge of God and fill herself with the knowledge God wishes to grant to souls through her agency.

"Before allowing his tongue to speak, the apostle

ought to raise his thirsting soul to God and then give forth what he has drunk in, and pour forth what he has been filled with," says St. Augustine.

St. Thomas tells us: "Those who are called to the works of the active life would be wrong in thinking that their duty exempts them from the contemplative life." This duty adds to it. Thus these two lives, instead of excluding each other, call for each other's help, implement and complete each other. Action to be productive has need of contemplation. The latter, when it gets to a certain degree of intensity diffuses some of its excess on the first.

. . . When there is need of speaking, we must not be afraid. He will tell us what and how to say the things He wants us to say.

Christ must be preached to pagans that they may know him, to heretics and schismatics that they may return to His fold; to bad Catholics that they may be drawn by His mercy; to the good and the pious that they may in His love be consumed and live His life.

Mary, under her divine Son, has sovereign dominion in the administration of supernatural graces and benefits of God's kingdom. She is our Mother because in her love she cooperated in our spiritual rebirth. She continues to be our Mother by nourishing the life of Christ in us.

Holiness increases in proportion to the devotion that one professes for Mary. The way back to God is through sinlessness and purity of life. Mary the Immaculate One is the way. She, "our life, our sweetness and our hope," is the way to peace. Pope Pius XII first consecrated the world to the Immaculate Heart of Mary on 31 October 1942. "There will be peace if the devotion to the Immaculate Heart of Mary is established throughout the world." This Our Lady promised to the three children of Fatima.

Charity must not remain shut up in the depth of the heart, for "no man lighteth a candle and putteth it under a bushel, but on a candlestick, that it may shine for all that are in the house."

A Missionary is a carrier of God's love, a burning light that gives light to all; the salt of the earth. It is said of St. Francis Xavier that "he stood up as a fire, and his words burnt like a torch." We have to carry Our Lord in places where He has not walked before. The Sisters must be consumed with one desire: Jesus. We must not be afraid to do the things He did—to go fearlessly through death and danger with Him and for Him.

A Missionary carries the interest of Christ continually in her heart and mind. In her heart there must be the fire of divine love and zeal for God's glory. This love makes her spend herself without ceasing. This becomes her real object in life and her joy. When Brother Lievens, S. J., was told to make his fire "a lasting one" he replied "No, I must make it a burning one." He spent himself in ten years' time. Jesus says: "Amen, unless the grain of wheat falls to the ground and dies, itself remaineth alone. But if it dies it brings forth much fruit". The Missionary must die daily if she wants to bring souls to God. The title "Missionary Religious" should humble us, for we are unworthy.

Our holy faith is nothing but a Gospel of love, revealing to us God's love for men and claiming in return man's love for God.

Let us "act" Christ's love among men, remembering the words of the Imitation, "love feels no burden, values no labors, would willingly do more than it can. It complains not of impossibilities, because it conceives that it may and can do all things; when weary is not tired; when straitened is not constrained; when frightened is not disturbed; but like a living flame and a torch all on fire, it mounts upwards and securely passes through all opposition."

Charity is patient, is kind, feels no envy, is never perverse or proud or insolent; it has no selfish aims, cannot be provoked, does not brood over an injury; it takes no pleasure in wrong-doing but rejoices over the victory of the truth; it sustains, believes, hopes, endures to the last. Love has a hem to her garment that reaches the very dust. It sweeps the stains from the streets and lanes, and because it can, it must. The Missionary of Charity, in order to be true to her name, must be full of charity in her own soul and spread that same charity to the souls of others, Christians and pagans alike.

Total surrender consists in giving ourselves completely to God, because God has given Himself to us. If God owes nothing to us and is ready to impart to us no less than Himself, shall we answer with just a fraction of ourselves? I give up my own self and in this way induce God to live for me. Therefore to possess God we must allow Him to possess our souls. How poor we would be if God had not given us the power of giving ourselves to Him. How rich we are now. How easy it is to conquer God. We give ourselves to Him, then God is ours, and there can be nothing more ours than God. The money with which God repays our surrender is Himself.

To surrender means to offer Him my free will, my reason, my own life in pure faith. My soul may be in darkness. Trial is the surest way of my blind surrender.

Surrender is also true love. The more we surrender, the more we love God and souls. If we really love souls, we must be ready to take their place, to take their sins upon us and expiate them. We must be living holocausts, for the souls need us as such.

There is no limit to God's love. It is without measure and its depth cannot be sounded. "I will not leave you orphans."

Now reverse the picture. There must be no limit to the love that prompts us to give ourselves to God, to be the victims of His unwanted love. We cannot be pleased with the common. What is good for others is not sufficient for us. We have to satiate the thirst of an infinite God dying of love. We cannot be content with the common lot, but with undaunted courage and fearlessness meet all perils and dangers with equanimity of soul, ever ready to make any sacrifice, to undertake any toil and labor. A Missionary of Charity must always push forward until she comes close to the King dying of thirst.

Loving trust. One thing Jesus asks of me is that I lean upon Him; that in Him alone I put complete trust; that I surrender myself to Him unreservedly. I need to give up my own desires in the work of my perfection. Even when I feel as if I were a ship without a compass, I must give myself completely to Him. I must not attempt to control God's actions. I must not desire a clear perception of my advance along the road, nor know precisely where I am on the way of holiness. I ask Him to make a saint of me, yet I must leave to Him the choice of that saintliness itself and still more the choice of the means that lead to it.

Cheerfulness should be one of the main points of our religious life. A cheerful religious is like sunshine in a community. Cheerfulness is a sign of a generous person. It is often a cloak that hides a life of sacrifice. A person who has this gift of cheerfulness often reaches great heights of perfection. Let the sick and suffering find us real angels of comfort and consolation. Why has the work in the slums been blessed by God? Not on account of any personal qualities but on account of the joy the Sisters radiate. What we have, faith and the conviction that we are the beloved children of God, people in the world have not got, much less the people in the slums. The surest way to preach Christianity to the pagan is by our cheerfulness. What would our life be if the Sisters were unhappy? Slavery and nothing else. We would do the work but we would attract nobody. This moodiness, heaviness, sadness, is a very easy way to tepidity, the mother of all evil.

If you are cheerful, have no fear of tepidity. Joy shines in the eyes, comes out in the speech and walk.

You cannot keep it in for it bubbles out. When people see the habitual happiness in your eyes, it will make them realize they are the loved children of God. Every holy soul at times has great interior trials and darkness, but if we want others to realize that Jesus is there, we must be convinced of it ourselves. Just imagine a Sister going to the slums with a sad face and heavy step. What would her presence bring to these people? Only greater depression.

Joy is very infectious; therefore, be always full of joy when you go among the poor. That cheerfulness, according to St. Bonaventure, has been given to man that he may rejoice in God in the hope of eternal good and at the sight of God's benefits; that he may rejoice in his neighbor's prosperity, take a delight in praising God and doing good works and feel disgust for all vain and useless things.

"It would be equally extraordinary," says St. Ignatius, "to see a religious who seeks nothing but God sad, as to see one who seeks everything but God happy."

Nationalism is inconsistent with our Constitution. Hence we should never fasten an unfavorable opinion on to people belonging to a nation other than ours. We must not defend politicians, nor should we make war and strife the subject of our conversation if mentioning them harms charity. . . . Nationalism is contrary to "Go therefore, and teach all nations" (Matthew 28:19). "Their sound hath gone forth to all the earth," St. Chrysostom says of St. Paul. "The heart of Paul is the heart of the whole world." Would that the same could be said of us. Girls of any nationality are welcome in our society.

Poverty. One loses touch with God when one takes hold of money. God preserve us. It is better to die. What would one do with surplus money? Bank it? We must never get into the habit of being preoccupied with the future. There is no reason to do so: God is there. Once the longing for money comes, the longing also comes for what money can give: superfluous things, nice rooms, luxuries at the table, more clothes, fans, and so on. Our needs will increase, for one thing leads to another, and the result will be endless dissatisfaction.

If you ever have to get things, you must buy things of cheaper quality. We must be proud of being poor. Pay attention to the little fox that sneaks in after us. We may carry water upstairs for a bath and find three buckets already full in the bathing room. Then the temptation comes to use all the water. . . .

If you have to sleep in a corner where there is no breeze, do not gasp and pant to show how much you feel it. In these little things one can practice poverty. Poverty makes us free. That is why we can joke and smile and keep a happy heart for Jesus. . . .

Some Sisters seem to be in a continual, feverish excitement about money for their work. Never give the impression to people when you beg that you are out to gather money. Let your work speak. Let your love for the people enkindle the rich people's hearts. They will give if you don't grab. Even if you have to beg, show that your heart is detached by being at ease, both when they refuse you and when they give.

A rich man of Delhi said: "How wonderful it is to see Sisters so free from the world, in the twentieth century when one thinks everything is old-fashioned but the present day."

Keep to the simple ways of poverty, of repairing your own shoes, and so forth, in short, of loving poverty as you love your mother. Our Society will live as long as that real poverty exists. The institutes where poverty is faithfully practiced are fervent and need not fear decay. We must always try to be poorer still and discover new ways to live our vows of poverty. We must think ourselves very fortunate if we get a few chances in life to practice this wonderful poverty. . . . To rejoice that others are more fortunate than we takes much virtue. . . .

When St. Francis of Assisi heard that a new rich house had been built for the brethren, he refused to enter the city. . . . We must not spend time and energy on the house by making it look attractive and beautiful. God save us from such convents where the poor would be afraid to enter lest their misery be a cause of shame to them.

When we dress ourselves we should with devotion remember what each article of the religious habit means to us: the sari with its blue band is a sign of Mary's modesty; the girdle made of rope is the sign of Mary's angelic purity; sandals are a sign of our own free choice; and the crucifix is a sign of love.

. . . Sisters shall live by begging alms. We depend entirely on the charity of the people. The Sisters should not be ashamed to beg from door to door if necessary. Our Lord Himself has promised a reward even for a cup of water given in His name. It is for His sake that we become beggars.

In fact He often endured real want, as the stories of the multiplication of the loaves and fishes and the plucking of the ears of corn on walks through the fields teach us. The thought of these instances should be salutary reminders whenever in the mission or at home our meals are meagre.... Our Lord on the cross possessed nothing.... He was on the cross that was given by Pilate. The nails and the crown were given by the soldiers. He was naked and when He died, cross, nails, and crown were taken away from Him. He was wrapped in a shroud given by a kind heart, and buried in a tomb that was not His. Yet Jesus could have died as a king and He could have risen from the dead as king. He chose poverty because He knew in His infinite knowledge and wisdom that it is the real means of possessing God, of conquering His heart, of bringing His love down to this earth.

Wholehearted free service. "What so ever you do to the least of my brethren, you do it to me. This is my commandment that you love one another." Suppress this commandment and the whole grand work of the church of Christ falls in ruins....

Charity for the poor must be a burning flame in our Society. And just as when a fire ceases to burn, it is no longer useful and gives no more heat, so the day the Society loses its charity toward the poor, it will lose its usefulness and there will be no life.

Charity for the poor is like a living flame. The drier the fuel, the brighter it burns; that is, when our hearts are separated from earthly motives and completely united to the will of God, we shall be able to give free service. . . . . The more united we are to God, the greater will be our love and readiness to serve the poor wholeheartedly. The more repugnant the work or the person, the greater also must be a Sister's faith, love, and cheerful devotion in ministering to Our Lord in this distressing disguise. . . .

When we recollect that in the morning we have held in our hands an all-holy God, we are more ready to abstain from whatever could soil their purity. Hence we should have deep reverence for our own person and reverence for others, treat all with accepted marks of courtesy, but abstain from sentimental feeling or ill-ordered affections. When we handle the sick and the needy we touch the suffering Body of Christ and this touch will make us heroic; it will make us forget the repugnance.

We need the eyes of deep faith to see Christ in the broken body and dirty clothes under which the most beautiful One among the sons of men hides. We shall need the hands of Christ to touch those bodies wounded by pain and suffering.

How pure our hands must be if we have to touch Christ's Body as the priest touches Him in the appearance of bread at the altar. With what love and devotion and faith he lifts the sacred host! These same feelings we too must have when we lift the body of the sick poor.

It is seeing that made Father Damien the apostle of

the lepers, that made St. Vincent de Paul the father
of the poor. . . . Such also was the case of St. Francis
of Assisi who, when meeting a leper completely disfigured, drew back, but then overcame himself and
kissed the terribly disfigured face. The result was that
St. Francis was filled with an untold joy, and the leper
walked away praising God for his cure. St. Peter
Claver licked the wounds of his Negro slaves. St. Margaret Mary sucked the pus from a boil. Why did they
all do these things if it was not because they wanted
to draw nearer to the heart of God. . . .

Spiritual life. "I kept the Lord ever before my eyes
because He is ever at my right hand that I may not
slip."

The true inner life makes the active life burn forth
and consume everything. It makes us find Jesus in the
dark holes of the slums, in the most pitiful miseries of
the poor, in the God-man naked on the cross, mourn-
ful, despised by all, the man of suffering, crushed like
a worm by the scourging and the crucifixion.

What does the Society expect of its members? To be
co-workers of Christ in the slums. Where will we fulfill
that aim? Not in the houses of the rich, but in the
slums. That is our kingdom. That is Christ's kingdom
and ours, the field we have to work in. If a boy leaves
his father's field and goes to work in another, he is no
longer his father's co-worker. Those who share everything are partners giving love for love, suffering for
suffering. Jesus, you hve given everything, life, blood,
all. Now it is our turn. We should put everything into
the field also.

. . . Our prayers should be burning words coming forth from the furnace of a heart filled with love.

. . . In our work we may often be caught in idle conversation or gossip. Let us be well on our guard for we may be caught while visiting families; we may talk about the private affairs of this or that one and so forget the real aim of our visit. We come to bring the peace of Christ but what if, instead, we are a cause of trouble? We must never allow people to speak against their neighbors. If we find that a family is in a bad mood and is sure to start their tale of uncharitableness, let us say a fervent prayer for them and say first a few things that may help them to think a little about God; then let us leave the place at once. We can do no good until their restless nerves are at peace. We must follow the same conduct with those who want to talk with the aim of wasting our precious time. If they are not in search of God, do not argue or answer their questions; leave them. Pray for them that they may see the light, but do not waste your time.

Hear Jesus your Co-Worker speak to you: "I want you to be my fire of love amongst the poor, the sick, the dying and the little children. The poor, I want you to bring them to me." Learn this sentence by heart and when you are wanting in generosity, repeat it. We can refuse Christ just as we refuse others.

"I will not give you my hands to work with, my eyes to see with, my feet to walk with, my mind to study with, my heart to love with. You knock at the door but I will not open. . . ." That is a broken Christ, a lame Christ, a crooked Christ deformed by you. If you give this to the people, it is all they will have. If you want

them to love Him, they must know Him first. Therefore, give the whole Christ, first to the Sisters, then to
the people in the slums, a Christ full of zeal, love, joy,
and sunshine.

Am I a dark light? a false light? a bulb without the
connection, having no current, therefore shedding no
radiance? Put your heart into being a bright light.

Holy Communion. If we want to have life and have
it more abundantly, we must live on the flesh of Our
Lord.

This needs no explanation, for who could explain
"the depth of the riches of the wisdom and knowledge
of God"? "How incomprehensible are His judgments,"
cried St. Paul, and "how unsearchable His way, for
who has known the mind of the Lord?"

... "O Lord God, give me grace this very day really
and truly to begin, for what I have done till now is
nothing...." The easiest form of self-denial is control
over our bodily senses ... that we may truly say with
St. Paul: "One thing I do, forgetting the things that
are behind and stretching forth myself to these that
are before, I press toward the mark...."

The danger for us is to forget that we are sinners.

Humility. Humility is nothing but truth. "What
have we got that we have not received?" asks St. Paul.
If I have received everything what good have I of my
own? If we are convinced of this we will never raise
our heads in pride.

If you are humble, nothing will touch you, neither
praise nor disgrace, because you know what you are.

. . . It is one thing for me to say I am sinner, but let someone else say that about me and then I feel it—I am up in arms.

If I am falsely accused, I may suffer, but deep down there is joy, because the correction is founded on reality, if even in the smallest way.

. . . Make it possible and even easy for your Superior to treat you and operate on you like the surgeon whose knife must cause pain in order to heal. When a sculptor carves a statue, what has he in his hand? A knife, and he cuts all the time.

Self-knowledge puts us on our knees, and it is very necessary for love. For knowledge of God gives love, and knowledge of self gives humility. St. Augustine says: "Fill yourselves first and then only will you be able to give to others." Self-knowledge is very necessary for confession. That is why the saints could say they were wicked criminals. They saw God and then saw themselves—and they saw the difference. Hence they were not surprised when anyone accused them, even falsely. . . . Each one of you has plenty of good as well as plenty of bad in her. Let none glory in her success but refer all to God.

We must never think any one of us is indispensable. God has ways and means. He may allow everything to go upside down in the hands of a very talented and capable Sister. God sees only her love. She may exhaust herself, even kill herself with work, but unless her work is interwoven with love it is useless. God does not need her work. God will not ask that Sister

how many books she has read, how many miracles she
has worked, but He will ask her if she has done her
best, for the love of Him. . . .

If you are discouraged it is a sign of pride, because
it shows you trust in your own powers. Never bother
about people's opinions. Be humble and you will never
be disturbed. Remember St. Aloysius, who said he
would continue to play billiards even if he knew he
was going to die. Do you play well? Sleep well? Eat
well? These are duties. Nothing is small for God.

. . . We have grown so used to each other that some
think they are free to say anything to anybody at any
time. They expect the Sisters to bear with their unkindness. Why not try first to hold your tongue? You
know what you can do, but you do not know how much
the other can bear.

Prayer: The interest of friendship that unites us,
that binds the young and old, is a chain of gold, a
thousand times stronger than flesh and blood, because
it permits the defects of the body and the vices of the
soul to be seen, while charity covers all, hides all, to
offer exclusively to admiration and love the work of
the hands of God. . . . He it is who in your old age
desires to decorate and adorn the fair beauty of your
soul with toil and grief. . . . To all the ills that assail
either heart or body hold up the shield of faith and
patience. In your old age you will complete for the
glory of God the tower of your soul that you began to
build in the golden days of your youth. And when He
comes, go forth to meet Him in the company of the
wise virgins, your lamp filled with oil and a flame.

Recreation is a means to pray better. Relaxation sweeps away the cobwebs in the mind. . . .

In one of her apparitions to St. Catherine Labouré, Our Lady had rings on every finger, from some of which rays shone forth while from the other rings no rays came. Our Lady explained that the rays were blessings granted by her to those who had asked for them, while the rayless rings represented graces that had not yet been asked for and given.

. . . In our Home for the Dying we understand better the value of a soul. The very fact that God has placed a certain soul in your way is a sign that God wants you to do something for him or her. It is not chance; it has been planned by God. We are bound in conscience to help him or her. When visiting the families you will meet with very much misery. Sometimes you will find a little child holding the head of the dead mother. It is then that you must use all your energy to help that little child in his sorrow.

Once there were found two little children near the dead body of their father, who had died two days before. . . . God will use you to relieve this suffering . . .

To prove that Christ was divine. . . .